WHAT DO YOU DO WHEN GOD STOPS WORKING?

A BIBLICAL REFLECTION ON SABBATH REST

BY KEITH RUCKHAUS

Wipf and Stock Publishers
Eugene OR

Wipf and Stock Publishers
199 West 8th Ave, Suite 3
Eugene OR 97401

When God Stops Working
By Keith Ruckhaus
Copyright c 2002 by Keith Ruckhaus
ISBN: 1-59244-090-8
Publication date: November, 2002

In remembrance of my dear friend Jack Bernard whose inspiration and encouragement was a major impetus for the making of this book.

CONTENTS

Foreward

Introduction   1

Chapter One - God's Gracious Turning   5
Shabbat Grounded in Creation – Genesis 1

     When Rest Began   6
     Holy and Bless - The Language of Rest   7
     Day, Image, Rule   10
     On Your Marks, Get Set, Stop!   12

Shabbat – Prescription for a Well-balanced Life   15
Shabbat in the Decalogue – Deuteronomy 5

     Shabbat's Foundation   15
     Shabbat – The Sure Sign of a Good Thing Going   17
     Prohibitions Against Confused Loyalties and Priorities   18
     Prohibitions Against False Representations   21
     Prohibitions Against Self-serving Manipulation   23
     Shabbat – Something to Hold on To   26
     The One to Make Shabbat Happen   30

The Truest Meaning of Rest   33
Jesus and Shabbat

     What Shabbat Had Come to Mean   33
     Showdown on Shabbat   35
     Shabbat Contraversy in Matthew   36
     The Good New Preached, Shabbat Restored   39
     The Burden of Rest   41
     The Lord of Rest – Mt.12:1-13   42
     It is Finished   47

God's Restless Rest   49
Hebrews 2-5

     Introduction – The Rest of Inconvenience   49
     Wilderness of Indecisions   52
     Two Way Wilderness - Choose your Phobia   54
     Sabbath Rest - Eternal Day has Begun   58
     Jesus – The Rising of the New Sabbath Day   62
     Jesus the Christ – The Perfect Situation   64
     Conclusion   71

Can Rest Be Done? 73
Thought on Shabbat

    Is There Such a Thing as a Day Off   74
    Out of the One   76
    Response to the False – Receiving Blessing   81
    Mercy, Mercy, Mercy   82
    Celebrating a Shabbat   85
    Shabbat – Rest in a Life Ordered by God   88
    Sum of All Fears – Boredom   90
    God Bless You   91

FOREWORD

The issue of Sabbath rest is one that has both theological and practical dimensions for both Jews and Christians. *Theologically,* it is part of a much larger question concerned with the relationship between Law and Gospel, between the Mosaic covenant and the covenant sealed in the blood of Jesus, between Church and synagogue, and between type and fulfillment. *Practically,* it has to do with how Christians relate to the Old Testament in our concrete daily lives. Do we ignore it? Do we pick and choose from it what we like? Do we embrace it as belonging to the Christian community and yet dismiss some of its clearest injunctions? How do we who celebrate Sunday, the Lord's day, the Day of Resurrection, deal with Shabbat? This is the question raised by Keith Ruckhaus. Does the Sabbath rest, which God gave to His people in the "old" covenant, still somehow speak meaningfully to us who have been grafted onto the People of God through Jesus Christ and who are justified in His blood?

We live in a culture that increasingly finds itself torn between the desire for leisure and the perceived necessity of constant work. How do rest and work relate to the ultimate questions of life? How do they relate to God? Is God completely indifferent to what we do with our time or does He have something to say to us in this regard? He certainly seems to have said something quite clearly to the people of Israel. What does that have to do with us today? Can Sabbath rest still somehow be received as a gift from God, a grace, even by those who live in the "new" covenant and who live in the modern age? If so, how? These are tough questions, but ones that we need to ponder.

To understand Christianity, it is necessary to see how deeply it is rooted in the Jewish tradition. The primary symbols that have created Christian identity – baptismal and eucharistic worship, structures and charisms of ministry, moral life, eschatological vision, and even Christ Himself – are incomprehensible except in relation to the Jewish inheritance of the Church. In other words, we cannot understand *who we are* except in relation to the People of Israel. While being constantly aware of the *novelty* of the work of God in Jesus Christ, the Christian tradition has also recognized its permanent indebtedness to the religious experience of the Jewish people and the revelation of God given through that experience.

Keith Ruckhaus's study of Sabbath rest stands within a long tradition of Christian thinkers trying to make sense of life today by relating it to the Jewish experience, as this is understood through the prism of Jesus Christ. It is an attempt to grasp and to reclaim what is permanent and universal in the

Jewish experience of Shabbat, while simultaneously seeing its fulfillment in the very person of Jesus. The basic theological and historical presupposition behind this position is that there is a living continuity between the synagogue, the temple and the Church, and that there is a genetic link between Christian worship and the liturgical tradition of Judaism. The new Christian "cult" does not replace or abolish the old Jewish "cult." It becomes the place where the permanent revelation of the Old Testament lives on in all its fullness. The new has meaning only on condition that the old is preserved.

Christians have long understood and defined the mystery of Christ in relation to Shabbat. Perhaps one of the clearest and most magnificent expressions of this is found in the Byzantine liturgical tradition at the celebration of the Matins of Holy Saturday:

> *The great Moses mystically foreshadowed this day, when he said: God blessed the seventh day. This is the Blessed Sabbath; this is the day of rest, on which the Only-Begotten Son of God rested from all His works. By suffering death to fulfill the plan of salvation, He kept the Sabbath in the flesh; by returning again to what He was, He has granted us eternal life through His resurrection, for He alone is good and the Lover of man.*

The value of Ruckhaus's work is that it calls on Christians to keep on exploring more and more deeply this relationship between the mystery of Christ and the work of God among His people of the Old Covenant. The full meaning, the mystical depth, of the Seventh Day as the day of rest and the day of fulfillment is located precisely in the mystery of Holy Saturday. Yet, without a sense of Shabbat, Holy Saturday would itself remain incomprehensible to us. The "old" Covenant conditions and shapes the "new", while the new reveals the depth and profundity of the old. Even when Christian theology had at times forgotten this, Christian worship maintained a lively sense of the connection.

Ruckhaus's reflection on the biblical *meaning* of the Sabbath rest draws us into this symbiotic relationship between old and new Covenants. It roots us in the history of primitive Christianity and its relationship with Judaism. In its own way, it reminds us once again that in its inner identity and reality, the Church of Jesus Christ is the People of God and the House of Israel abroad throughout the world.

Fr. Chrysostom Frank
St. John Vianney Seminary

INTRODUCTION

Some time ago, a good friend asked me if I could write something on rest. I, as well as a small group of others, had just come out of a church debacle that left most of us torn, exhausted, confused, and worn through with a painful experience. This was the impetus behind this writing. At the time, we all sensed a deep need for a season in which we could be renewed, refreshed, revived or restored in God. The church that we were a part of was geared towards always going, going, going. Stopping our work, was almost considered a sin. It was viewed as a kind of laziness or spiritual lethargy. Having lived that way for many years, it seemed necessary for many of us to change our thinking as well as our lifestyle to experience God's rest.

Originally, this was just going to be for the little group of leftovers, but I offered it out to a broader audience. Also originally, I had planned on writing a brief essay. I haven't been very good at being brief, and now look what I got myself into. The more I go along the more I wonder how much rest my friend will experience from any of what I'm writing. Somehow rest or peace seems to get bogged down in complexity and then it doesn't seem quite so restful anymore. As with any theological treatise, it is a part of the big soup, and cannot be partaken of in isolation without losing its flavor. I do wonder, as I continue, whether any rest will be had in all of this?

It does seem funny to me how in our society, the notion of rest alludes us. It is something we have to know conceptually, because we don't actually experience it. So, immediately, there is something that is ineffectual about any treatise of rest. My friend, as well as many others, are looking for a real, physical, and abiding rest. To get some idea of rest may not seem very helpful. Many of us feel overworked. There is too much going on in our lives. At home, the pace doesn't let up. An acquaintance of my wife informed her that she and her family practically live out of their car. They eat, clothe, have family meetings, and do business and homework in it. With the added introduction of the Internet, the market now never closes. Somebody must be working at all times. To interject some conceptual notion of a slow-down constituted by God in all of that, doesn't seem to fit.

We, of course, take our leisure very seriously, and there are plenty of profiteers of pleasure to choose from. So too, our days off can often be more anxious and exhausting than work. The pursuit of tickets, reservations, and parking for entertainment can deplete our patience as well as our wallets. Feeling worn-out and sore from recreational sport provides a physical sense of rest for many. God's Sabbath rest, however, has nothing to do with the search for self-fulfilling leisure; indeed, it is counter to it.

I do believe that there is simplicity in God's rest, in Sabbath rest; but it is in the midst of our world as we know it, not in a negation of it or escape from it. Neither is it found in working ourselves silly in an attempt to control the elements outside ourselves, to hold chaos back. This is precisely what idolatry is about. We end up in never ending contractual negotiations with the powers. Like the sports contracts of our day, so it is with contractual agreements with powers; they can change or be nullified willy-nilly.

In the middle of a formless, worthless, chaotic universe God places the earth (Gen.1:2). The Lord intentionally took a people for Himself out of the land of perpetual work and strategically placed them in the middle of the nations. The Shabbat command is in the middle of the Ten Words, weeding through the false notions of relationship to gods on the one hand and destructive human relations on the other. Even more so, it bridges the seemingly impossible chasm between God and man.

So, it shouldn't be a surprise to us - although it always is - that Jesus speaks of rest most profoundly under the shadow of assassination, in the heat of controversy, in the middle of opposition, and in the treacherous mine field of revolutionary fervor. It is here where Jesus promises us that we will have many troubles. Matter of fact, Jesus tells us to expect it, but he doesn't stop there, for he announces again and again that there is a monumental turning point of history happening in him. Jesus is confident that if anyone understood this, it would bring rest. It is in the one thing that God places in the middle that is the center-piece for life's blessing. Out of the one, the many are blessed.

Understanding that Sabbath rest is at the center of things and at the heart of life is carried one step further by the early church. Because of the on-going and very real life of the ascended Jesus, they understood there to be another Sabbath rest that is yet to be experienced, a destination to be journeyed to. Finally, the Sabbath rest found in Jesus stands right in the middle of temporal and eternal time.

Perhaps there is some idea of rest that many of us need to be reintroduced to or reminded of in a new way. I have found this study of Sabbath rest to have slowly seeped into my being. There is something profound and fundamental to be understood about God and our relationship with him in Sabbath rest. I still find it quite the struggle to experience a rest in God on a regular basis, but I am also finding that I am clearer than before on what to look for and what is important about God's rest. For some, it may be helpful to affirm that there is a resting place in God. God wants it for you, and you need not feel ashamed or guilty that He wants you to take a break. Ultimately, Shabbat is about taking a break from a world that now says, "Don't stop till you get enough," and entering God's world that says, "Enough! It is finished, and it is good."

Introduction

May God bless you, and may you find His Sabbath rest.

GOD'S GRACIOUS TURNING
Shabbat Grounded in Creation – Genesis 1

Recently, I came across a couple of ads that appeal to what is an important value and need in our contemporary culture. A local phone company has taken on a slogan to push a new communications devise: "We never stop working for you." The product for sale would provide an always-available stream of endless distraction: games, entertainment updates, and trivial information pursuits. A well-known burger business was pushing their new late night service. On a billboard, there is a large picture of French fries with a slogan above it: "Because desire keeps no time tables" How true of our world.

With these two examples I am confronted with what is perhaps a dominant idea inherent in our social psyche. We are most happy when our lives and our things are going all the time. The world works best when it keeps on working.

Perhaps it is not like this in some cultures today, but I know of one culture that sees things differently. That is God's culture. From the first chapter of the Bible, we are informed that a work stoppage is in fact at the center of life. This account in no way renounces the necessity and the pleasure of work, but it simply doesn't give work the exclusive and center stage to meaningful human existence. In fact, Shabbat is God's announcement that it is just the opposite: it is in the ceasing that fulfillment resides.

Let me just come straightaway with the answer to the question proposed in the title of this book. One should find a double message in it. For many who struggle with believing in God, it is quite common to put God to the pragmatic test, "God, if you do this one thing for me, I'll believe and trust in you." It is pretty harmless to see if God works or not. It is not, on the other hand, a very effective test. God may, in fact, intensely desire to prove Himself to an inquiring soul, yet he could do this not so much in doing something for a person but in His refusal to do so. It is often the case at my household that I finally sit down after a whirlwind of activity. "Ahh! Time to take a break," I affirm to myself. Predictably, one of the children will come at that instant and request my energies to be applied somewhere, "Dad could you do this for me?" "No," I reply, "I just sat down. I'm not doing anything right now." God, in fact, can have a similar posture.

There is a notion that perhaps has become completely foreign to us: God stops working. He ceases. He rests, reposes, reclines. Even more so, he has woven that part of Himself into the very fabric of creation and our human existence. Life will not make sense without ceasing times.

I had a sixth grade student who had his difficulties getting on task in my class. Once he finally got started, however, he would have an almost trance-like focus on his work. Unless I could catch it early, he would be glued to his seat while everyone else had moved on to the next class. Perhaps our sophisticated society reveals the same embarrassment as my student. We can get so wound up in activity that we haven't noticed that everyone else has finished. It is time for us to learn anew that God ceases from his labors. What do you do when God stops working? You stop working also. In that hallowed break, something of God, our world and us are to be discovered and revisited.

When Rest Began

One of the clearest biblical notions of rest is under the rubric of Shabbat[1]. It is encountered immediately in the first chapter of the Bible. Indeed, it could be argued that the main purpose of the creation account isn't so much to explain how creation came about, but rather, what is so important about Shabbat.

> *God looked over all that he had made. Wow! It was really good! It was morning and evening the sixth day.*
> *And God completed the heavens and the earth and every assembly piece that went with it to set it on its way. On the seventh day, since God had masterfully completed everything he was working on, he stopped working. On the seventh day God stopped working. God blessed the seventh day and set it apart, when on that day he stopped doing the work of creating.*[2]

God stopped working; this is Shabbat. Unlike us, however, God stopped because there was nothing left to do. God had completely, masterfully, intricately created everything. Already, we have a big reason why, we do not often feel restful; we never have a sense that our work is done. But God didn't stop doing on the seventh day; he just stopped doing work. Said

---

[1] There is no significance implied by employing the Hebrew transliteration – Shabbat – instead of the standard English pronunciation - Sabbath. In cases where the word is being used as an adjective instead of a noun, it works better to use Sabbath i.e. Sabbath rest instead of Shabbat rest.
[2] Gen.1:31-2:4 ; my translation

God's Gracious Turning

another way, on the seventh day God stopped working on creation and started doing something else. So, to understand rest, we need to go on to see what God did on Shabbat.

Holy and Bless - The Language of Rest

There is a certain language around Shabbat that can guide our understanding and perhaps lead us to some rest. Here, I want to interject something that is important. It has to do with how to understand the Bible - hermeneutics, but also with how one views God – theology. Simply put, it is important to pay attention to the language of the text. Essentially, listen to the words God has spoken.

Our God is not a telephone-talking or talk-show-jabbering kind of communicator. He is a God who speaks with deliberation and force. He is a master communicator. His choice of words is not haphazard or casual. I really believe this. His vocabulary is deliberate and rich with nuance. In the study of hermeneutics, there is a notion called "dynamic equivalence". It is the idea of transferring biblical words and concepts into contemporary language. This has its value, but it has its dangers. One danger is that we can stray away from God's language, his vocabulary. We can lose the kind of connection with God that is like when you are told a joke but then the punch line is said in another language. When someone translates it for you – dynamic equivalence – it doesn't seem all that funny. The translator then informs you that your language really can't say it quite the same way.

What is to follow is an exploration into the language of Shabbat. The hope is that if we listen to the words of Shabbat, of rest, we might experience rest. I advocate that we ought to let God's language seep into ours rather than our language seeping into God's.

The language of rest is creation language. This is appropriately so because Shabbat is not something imposed on the created order, but is its most critical element. The passage quoted above – Genesis 1:31-2:4 – is cumulative. It closes off and finishes the tightly constructed creation account that starts out the book of Genesis, the Torah, and indeed our entire Bible. "In the beginning" (v1:1) ends when God stops (v2:2). God started creating and then he finished, Shabbat.

The Sabbath declaration not only closes chapter one. It also plays a critical role in introducing chapter two as well as the rest of Genesis. It is critically intermediary. Indeed it is conciliatory and packed with theological daring. It takes on the task of harmonizing two theological perspectives that may appear in conflict with each other. Genesis one presents God, Elohim, as the master of the universe. Elohim controls the cosmos as well as all the natural elements. Chapter two presents the Lord, Yahweh who is an intense relational God actively involved in the affairs of the human race. The first four verses of chapter two are meant to subordinate chapter two to one. Genesis one and two are not parallel accounts of creation. In fact, chapter two is not a creation account; rather, it is the "unfolding of the history of mankind as the intended offspring of the creation of the heavens and the earth."[3] It is the seventh day that is the christening of God's covenant activity. The seventh day ushers in God's creative activity into man's history. As Von Rad states, "To talk of an 'institution of the Sabbath' would be a complete misappropriation of the passage. It is God who rests. It tells something about Yahweh and his relation to creation. It is in fact a particularly mysterious and gracious turning towards his creation."[4] Again, the language of rest is the language of creation and covenant. It masterfully weaves two notions that had not fit together very well in Israel's early history, that their God is both Creator and Saviour. The language of creation found in Genesis one is this: separate (holy), fill, day, complete, and image. All these lead to and are encompassed in the word **baruch** – blessing. These are the words to be explored.

The first key word to look at in the language of rest is found in Gen. 2:3. The word is **qadesh** - holy. The word is a verb; it is something God did. God was still doing things on Shabbat. He *holisized* the seventh day. Essentially, what God did was separate the seventh day from the other six. He set it apart. Although the scripture places **qadesh** after blessing, it is actually its precursor. For this biblical writer, God has to first separate before he can bless. For the writer of Genesis one, this is an important theological point; that is, out of the one, many are blessed.

This notion is expounded in the liturgical style of Genesis 1. The first three days of creation are days of separation. God first separates light from darkness, then the expanse, and finally the waters. The end result of this series of separations is *eretz* – land. The author wants to show that the way God brought forth the earth is the same way that God brought forth a people. Out of all the vast array of the creation elements, the earth is the one place that God has extracted or extruded out of the rest to be the place of his intentional and intensified creative activity.

Likewise, the intention of Genesis is to demonstrate how out of all the families of the world God pulled one out, to be the object of His activity. The emphasis on the earth comes out as immediately as the second verse of the Bible. Verse one gives a sweeping statement about God's creative

---

[3] Brevard Childs, *Introduction to the Old Testament as Scripture*, pg 149, Fortress Press
[4] Gerhard Von Rad, *Old Testament Theology Vol.I*, pg 147-148, Harper and Row Publishers

activity. It simply states: God created it all. By putting the subject –earth- in front of the verb –was- in the second verse, the author deliberately draws attention to the earth as the intensified concern of God. The first three days is a reductionist activity of God. Like when one extrudes strawberries until it becomes the essence of the fruit – jelly, so God did with all the elements of creation to make the earth. This is the deliberate set up of Genesis chapter one. The first three days of creation were meant to demonstrate that God separates before he blesses. God sets apart a special place for his intentional and intensified activity – His love.

As the first three days provide the place for God's covenant activity, the earth, the next three days provide the object of this activity. The end result is ***adam*** – man. Here the notion of blessing is introduced. In the second set of three days God commands that the thing that had been separated now be filled. So, the arena of light is now to be filled with lights. Then, the expanses are to teem with swarming things. Finally, the earth is to multiply with living things. What God reduced to essence in the first three days, ***qadesh*** (holy), he expands – fills out and multiplies – in the next three days, ***baruch*** (blessing). We are to take note of what in particular is blessed. It is living creatures, those who are able to be fruitful, multiply, and fill. Here, we have our definition of bless. It is an empowerment or endowment to bring living to fullness or completion. Blessing is endowed with purpose; it is driven and compelled toward expressing that biblical affirmation, "On the seventh day, God completed everything."

Inherent in the definition of bless is its purpose. Blessing is not a self-acquiring activity. To be blessed means to be empowered to bless. Out of the one, many are blessed. God pulls one out of the many, and that one becomes the object of God's special activity. God blesses that one, not for the purpose of having it over everyone else, but for being the source of blessing for many others. Blessing begets blessing. To bless means not only to declare something good, but also to destine it for goodness and fullness. Blessing means to empower blessing.

Out of the one, many are blessed. God blessed the seventh day and made it holy. Holiness and blessing, separation and fullness, set apart and fruitfulness, one and many, extrude and expand, this is the language of creation. Both of these words, holy and bless (keep in mind that they are both verbs), are synthesized into one word, Shabbat – cease. When God stops, being picked out for blessing starts. The grammatical emphasis in 2:3 stresses the point that the seventh day was made holy and blessed in that God stopped working on that day. There is a beautiful twist in all of this. As I have tried to show, setting apart (holy) and filling out (blessing) were indeed the creative activities of the first six days. The difference is that in the first six days, separating and filling was done via God's word. God spoke separation and blessing. On the seventh day, the essential acts of creating continue; only now, it is not in word but in rest, not in speaking but in ceasing. Holiness and blessing occurred on the seventh day because God stopped working. It does sound odd, but it is true that things can be accomplished even if one is not doing anything. Things can happen even when one is not trying to 'make it happen'.

Genesis 2:2-4 brings a powerful closure to the creation account. At the beginning, chaos ruled the earth. Unlike us modern scientific types, the ancients were not obsessed with the question of how did all this come into being and how did we get here? What dominated their thinking was a more pressing question; is the cosmos and our existence in it essentially one of chaos, randomness, and disarray? Does chaos rule? Does existence have any purpose or meaning?

The creation account attempts to bring home a powerful theological point summed up in the statement on Shabbat. The answer is a resounding and emphatic NO! The earth is not moving towards chaos, but towards completeness, order, and rest. It is moving towards God because God has graciously turned toward it. There is a profound proclamation in God's ceasing on the seventh day. **God has intentionally and graciously turned toward his creation.** Regardless of what the world has become, Shabbat is God's resounding affirmation of his creation. God's face shines toward us. Here, I will explore some more language of creation to understand how holiness and blessing come together in Shabbat.

Day, Image, and Rule.

Are the heavens and earth essentially random? Is there no form, shape or order? No! Because the very first act of creation is that God made day. It is easy to figure out that the creation of the first day was to set the framework for the rest of creation. God needed day to do his work. We should understand the Hebrew word for day –*yom*- as a framework of time, which is one of its primary uses in Hebrew. The very first thing God did was bring order to the seemingly random elements of the cosmos. The creation of day immediately reverses the formless nature of primal creation. It sets apart, makes things distinguishable. Holiness answers shapelessness. Light subdues darkness by making distinctions. Light separates darkness into day and night and takes away its formidable power. The scary nature of randomness is now given order. On the first day, God set purpose into creation.

Are the heavens and earth essentially empty and in disarray? Again the answer is no! God fills out what has been empty and worthless. God fills the expanse above with lights. This filling out of sky serves first to be a sign. The word sign means to mark, pledge, token, or memorialize. Its purpose is to fill out day with appointed times and seasons. The second function of lights is to govern, rule. The word here is **mashal**. It basically means alongside, to be next to. Its prominent use in the Hebrew is not rule, but it is a wisdom word. It is translated into Greek as **parabolos** – parable. It carries a notion of balance. The lights are to rule by representation; they parallel or reflect the light of day.

God continues to fill the expanses with living moving creatures. Here the emphasis is on teeming, moving, living creatures. The creatures are **nephesh**, often translated soul. It means "open throated"; creatures are those with the capacity to take in life. Only creatures can be blessed because only they have the capacity to confer abundant and effective life. The governing aspect of day four is carried forth into the next day in that the creatures are divided into their kinds. They are given distinction and boundaries.

The filling out of creation reaches its culmination in the creation of God's image bearers – **adam**. This is not the pinnacle of creation, but its lowest point. For Adam is the last creature and the most dependant; nevertheless, God blesses them. Here again the empowerment to fill out creation includes a governing function. The blessed one is an image bearer. It is that one who not only is blessed but also has the capacity to bless, to make blessing happen. We can take note of this in Genesis chapter 5. Seth is the image of Adam. This is a statement to indicate his special status as the blessed one of Adam. He bears the image because he is blessed and endowed with the power to bless.

Here again, this is where filling, multiplying, and rulership come together. It is interesting to note that image here does not serve to give form to creation, but to fill it. This may not seem like much, but it may in fact critically address the idols of pagans. The emphasis is on their shape and form. Godly image doesn't bring order or purpose as much as it brings worth and meaning. True image is life giving, and it can't be equated with form. The blessed one is image-bearer because that one has the endowment to be life giving. Out of the one, the many are blessed; this is true image. This is what should rule creation.

There is one final creation word to complete our consideration; it is **qalah** - complete. In verse 2:1, the verbs *complete* and *cease* are paralleled. There is a difference of opinion on this, but I go with the idea that creation wasn't finished **until** the seventh day. If this is so, it means that what closed off creation was when God stopped working. Shabbat – to stop working – was the finishing touch to creation. The catch twenty-two is that the work of creation on the seventh day is when God stopped working. (If this is true, it is no wonder why we moderns don't understand rest. We have no notion of work going on without us doing work). The activity of creation continues on the seventh day. The idea is repeated for emphasis; it is because God stopped working that the seventh day was set apart, blessed, and complete. When God stopped working, all that is left is God. A satisfied, marveling God in the midst of his creation is ultimately what makes Shabbat.

Is it helpful to have an image of a reclining and simply satisfied God? I lived in a neighborhood that was heavily populated by Mexicans. There is one thing I always admired about them. On any given Sunday, you can see them out on their front or back porch, in chairs or lying in the grass with plenty of food and drink. They were there all day, satisfied, content, resting. The hard work of the week is gone for one day. I can imagine our God sometimes in the midst of that.

On the seventh day, God rests in this; now there is a place, earth, and an object, man, for his intensified covenant activity, that is his love. God has made all, is satisfied with all, and has turned towards all. Certainly, the earth and mankind especially have caused God a whole lot of unrest; nevertheless, the passage is God's emphatic affirmation. God's face is turned towards us. Rest is found when we understand that we are in the right arena of God's gracious activity and that we are the special objects of His love. God has turned towards his creation and has never stopped turning towards it (even when he regretted it). In God, purpose and meaning are in every aspect of our existence. This is rest – out of the one many are blessed.

On Your Marks, Get Set, Stop!

Shabbat means to cease or stop, and in particular in means to stop working. There is something marvelous that happened when God stopped working. When God stopped doing the work of creation, he started His gracious and redemptive work towards us. When I am teaching, I sometimes find it necessary to stop and give a hard and intensified glance at a particular student who is not being attentive. For the student, it is not a particularly welcome or comfortable turning in their direction. There is, however, a similar kind of glance that has quite the opposite affect, like when a lover first turns his attention to one he is interested in. That glance, equal in intensity as mine towards a student, excites wonderment, adrenalin, and thrill as the receiver gloats in a marvelous realization. He looked at me! He favors me! On the seventh day, God interrupted creation to let his face shine upon it.

There is another way to say all of this. On the first six days, the heavens and the earth began and came into being. On the seventh day, God's relentless grace began and entered the history of mankind.

We must learn or be reminded of a simple truth. We too must stop working to find grace. It must be a daily thing, and not just something reserved for the

God's Gracious Turning

seventh day or special seasons. We must also learn, however, that Shabbat is not counter to creation; it is an intragal part of it. It is a mistake to struggle too hard to find rest because it is woven into the very nature of things. Shabbat is not about picking a fight with the world, but affirming what God has affirmed about it. Essentially and ultimately, God says and is still saying, "It is good".

The world I live in seems to press in harder and harder with the message, "Don't stop till you get enough." It seems to keep making a longer and longer list of necessary items. I'm not just talking about material things. The pressure increases that we must be on a ceaseless vigil to be informed, educated, and aware. We must be tireless watchman, or we'll die out.

If we want to enter into God's Sabbath rest, then we must learn to shut down and shut up the busy-ness. We need times and seasons when we ignore what our little world says is so bloody important or necessary. We need to make time for saying to ourselves, to God, and to our neighbor what is fundamentally important to any and all thriving on this planet; it is to bask in the warm and radiant light of His unfailing love.

The Many Gifts of God

When woman and man were made,
God left one good thing for last: the day to give thanks for the
world and its wonders.
Now the seventh day has come. Now Shabbat begins:

> *To bring us rest, to bring us joy;*
> *to bring us song, to bring us peace.*

How good it is, how filled with beauty!
On this day we remember the goodness of all creation.

On this day we remember the goodness of earth,
water and sun, and all that grows.

On this day we remember the many gifts of God.
Let us remember, and let us give thanks.[5]

---

[5] *Gates of Prayer* pg 262 Central Conference of American Rabbis

Shabbat – Prescription for a Well-balanced Life
Shabbat in the Decalogue - Deuteronomy 5

Shabbat is God's gracious affirmation of and intention for his creation, but it is readily apparent that the world is not so interested in that. From ancient times until now, humankind has stepped in with its own agenda. The world is not at all interested in stopping. It doesn't believe that you can thrive without strife. We all have the voices that barrage us with messages of fear, anxiety, and doubt. They tell us that we cannot stop working or we will diminish, lose out, be homeless, or die. We are presented with a relentless parade of images that remind us that chaos is weakly restrained and the powers are restless and demanding. It is, for me, a dreadful venture to watch T.V. commercials. The images that are presented of us are disturbing. They present the most petty, vain, and arrogant desires as necessities that only a fool would do without. It certainly does seem viable that the idea of a work stoppage, of a ceasing time, is contrary to the law of survival.

This issue is masterfully addressed in the Ten Words given to Moses and the Israelites. If nothing else, the Words at least acknowledge that Shabbat, God's rest, has its difficulties. Yet, even here, Shabbat is God's positive and gracious affirmation that He is in this very situation. God strategically places the Shabbat command smack dab in the center of this apparent tension with a restless world. It seeks to strip away false notions of demanding gods, powers, and images, on the one hand, and destructive ideas about human relations on the other. The two positive and particular commands, observe Shabbat and honor your father and mother, are placed in the middle of prohibitions concerning relationships with "gods" and humans; they serve as the critical juncture between them.

The Shabbat's Foundation – The Creative and Redemptive work of Grace

A major source to explore Sabbath rest is, of course, in the fourth commandment of the Decalogue.

> *In order to keep the Sabbath day separate, as the Lord your God commanded you, work six days and do everything necessary to make a living. However, the seventh day is a ceasing time by the Lord your God; in it you shall stop working. This applies not only*

> *to you but also to your son, daughter, male and female servants, ox and donkey, and even any of your immigrants who stay with you. Do this so that all who labor for you may rest as well as you. And you shall remember that you were a slave in the land of perpetual work (Egypt), and the Lord your God brought you out of there by a mighty hand and an outstretched arm; therefore, the Lord your God commanded you to observe Shabbat.*[6]

In the two accounts of the Decalogue – Exodus 20 and Deut.5 – there are different reasons given to observe Shabbat. The Exodus account grounds it in creation, but the Deuteronomic version grounds it in a miraculous act of deliverance. These are not contrary or competing versions. As I said in the Genesis commentary, the Sabbath verses are a deliberate and successful attempt at synthesizing creation theology with humankind's history. Long before Cain, Lemech, Bable, and the degenerative march of history, God had already placed his stamp of approval on the good intention of it all. These Biblical writers do not see that God is against the world. His face is turned towards it, and the completed work of creation expressed in Shabbat is also the germination of God's activity in mankind's history. **Fact: God's creative activity has been and is being worked out in history.** We will discover that the language of Shabbat found in the creation account, *separate, cease, image, likeness, rest, work, goodness,* is reiterated in the Decalogue.

Shabbat in the Decalogue is grounded in another complete and gracious work initiated solely by God. *I am the Lord your God, who brought you out of the land of Egypt, out of the house of slavery.* Perhaps another way to say this is: *you have been saved by grace, and this is none of your own doing, lest you have some reason to boast.* The word – brought out- means to go out of or extrude. It is used in the sense of germinate or burst forth like the first sprig bursting from its planted seed. From this idea comes the noun form that is often translated *source or origin.* Already in this phrase we see a similar notion of God's creative work, that of separation. The vision of human society – and we should understand the Decalogue as visionary – is preceded by a work of separation. God pulled out one people from the many to be the intensified object of his loving, creative, and redemptive activity. Out of the one, the many are blessed.

This verse functions as a precursor to the Decalogue in a similar way as the first day of creation. The creation of light sets up the rest of the days leading to its completion. God pulls Israel out of the land of perpetual work in order to set up his redemptive activity. God's salvation work is the light by which he does his work in history. The separation of light from darkness does not lead to the trashing of all that is not light. Light makes for the rest of creation

---

[6] Deuteronomy 5:12 – 15; my translation

to happen. So also, God separates a people from the others, not to condemn or trash them, but so his creative activity will happen in the world. All this to say, salvation and being separated are not for the purpose of condemning the world but for affirming and redeeming it. Here again is something critical about understanding rest. It is grounded in a solid understanding that God has graciously turned towards the world.

Shabbat – The Sure Sign of a Good Thing Going

It may be hard for the modern reader of the Ten Words[7] to immediately appreciate the central placement of the Sabbath word. Along with the word to honor parents, the Sabbath command is pronounced in positive terms and is centrally located in the Ten Words. This deliberate placing has a meaning in and of itself. For the ancient mindset, a right idea must be in symmetry; it must be balanced. This is most clearly demonstrated in the proverbs. No statement, in and of itself, is meaningful unless it has a counter statement. It is the two statements put together that provides the meaning of both. Actually, the heart of the meaning, the true wisdom, is considered to be between them. It is in the convergence of the two counter-weights at the center that they balance out.

It is easy to spot in the Ten Words that two main concerns are being addressed. The first three commands address the covenant community's relationship with their God and other gods, and the last five commands address relationships within the covenant community. The two major concerns converge in the middle with the Sabbath word and the command to honor parents. In a sense, the last five words are meant to be a mirrored image of the first three. Like when one stands before a mirror, the real thing is accurately reflected in the mirrored image. The Shabbat and honoring parent commands serve as the convergence of the real and the mirrored image, like when a person touches her hand to the mirror. The two middle imperatives are the point of contact between God and his covenant people.

The centrality of the middle commands, especially Shabbat, means neither that it is the most important nor the most comprehensive of the Ten Words. The first and the last Word serve that purpose, and the other commands work from opposite directions towards the center with a more narrow and specific injunction. Like when a magnifying glass can increasingly narrow light until it comes to a concentrated pinpoint of light and heat, so it is with the Ten

---

[7] The Ten Words are what the Hebrew Bible calls them; hence, they are more than just commands. They should speak to us. They are instructive which is why it is called 'torah': teaching.

Words. The Sabbath Word, coupled with the Word to honor parents, is the Ten Words in a concentrated form. They provide a focus to the whole.[8]

The Sabbath Word therefore becomes the most critical element of the Ten Words[9], so much so, that it is called the "sign of the covenant." Moses enjoins the Israelites to take observing Shabbat seriously. "This will be a sign between me and you for the generations to come."[10] Having some kind of visible tangible object as a pledge or reminder of a covenant relationship is a critical notion in the ancient world. Although a signature on a contract could be a point of comparison for us, it must be realized that for the ancient world, a sign is much more than that.

It is the clearest measure of how the covenant is going. Be reminded that all the heavenly lights are signs (Gen.1:14). As previously discussed, the sun and moon are signs because they lead, rule, or guide. Also implied in a sign is the quality of absolute reliability. The North Star has been the ultimate trustworthy sign for seafarers to this day. It is a real, visible guide that governs and determines how and when sea travelers operate. So too, the Shabbat is the North Star of the Decalogue. It was considered the clearest indicator of the well-being of all involved. With this in mind, it is as Breuggeman observes, "No wonder the Israelites took great pains to get it right!"[11] Keeping in mind the central placement of the Sabbath Word and the Word to honor parents, it is valuable to see how the other Words lead to them.

Prohibitions Against Confused Loyalties and Priorities
Do not have for yourself other gods before me.
Do not covet and desire what belongs to your neighbor.[12]

In a very clear sense, we can understand the first and the tenth Words as summary and comprehensive of all ten. It was well established that to love God wholeheartedly and your neighbor as yourself accurately summed up the covenant stipulations expressed in the Ten Words.[13] Even though the

---

[8] A close connection between the Sabbath and the social importance of a father and mother is seen clearly in the attempts of Nehemiah and Ezra to reconstitute Israel after the exile: Neh. 10:31-32, Neh. 13:15-27, Ezra 10:3ff.

[9] 'Human Sabbath: A study in Deuteronomic Theology' Princeton Seminary Bulletin, by Patrick Miller, Bulletin 6 1985 PG 81-97. "I am convinced it occupies a very central place and plays a significant role in Deuteronomic theology."

[10] Exod. 31:12, see also Neh.9:13-14 and Ezek. 20:20

[11] Old Testament Theology by Walter Breuggeman, pg 191

[12] In the text above, I am providing a shortened version of each Word. For a thorough reading of the commands refer to Deuteronomy 5:7-21 and Exodus 20:2-17.

[13] Mark 12:28-31

Shabbat – Prescription for a Well-balanced Life

wording of the first and the tenth Word are different, they are after the same problem. It appears that these two Words get as much at motivation as to action. This is true, but be reminded; they are both addressing a serious and over arching problem that ruins any relationship, whether god or man. It is the problem of wanting to posses and control a relationship. It is an attitude that views critical social relationships necessary for living only as a vehicle for acquisition.

We should immediately notice something about the first Word. Before the Israelites get on with trying to do or not do something, they should readily acknowledge a powerful reality. Yahweh is present: *other gods before me*. The Hebrew expression, literally "upon my face", is the common way to express presence. Indeed, if someone is "in your face" you pretty much know that he is there. The Israelites are already before God meaning that he is the sole ruler, sovereign and rightful owner of all that the Israelites have. If this reality were profoundly understood, then there would be no need to have other gods alongside Yahweh's presence. It is best to understand *other gods* as unknown or strange. In other words, the Lord does not know these gods. He is neither related to them, nor does he have a relationship with them. Indeed, He needs no relationship with them; therefore, God's people do not need them either.

The Lord, clearly and succinctly, prohibits his people from having unknown gods. Fundamentally, this is a prohibition against thinking any god is a possession, a matter of acquisition or a vehicle for it. Even more so, the emphasis is on having strange gods "for yourself". In a way, it would be an insult for the Israelites to think to house foreign deities without Yahweh knowing about it. In this regard, perhaps the Lord experiences something similar to my experience teaching middle school. One thing I found hard to get used to is when there is misbehavior right before my eyes, and then when I address it with the offender, they present themselves as naively innocent of such violations. On top of the original problem, I'm confronted with the extra subtle offense that she thinks I'm too dumb to figure out what just happened before my eyes. What is behind this example and the problem of confused deities is shear presumption. It presumes that competing loyalties is no big deal and that the Lord doesn't mind.

There are two consistent and clear expressions of this violation in the history of Israel. It becomes clear that the Israelites rarely thought of the other gods replacing Yahweh as their god. They just underestimated to what extent the relationship with the Lord required exclusive loyalty. First, there was the problem of the "high places". The gods associated with them were the local Canaanite gods. The presumption around retaining these deities was that although Yahweh was a ruler of all, he wasn't to be bothered with petty local affairs. He only deals with the big stuff. Making political alliances with foreign rulers and their deities was the second way the Israelites violated this command. Beginning with Solomon, this policy was acquiescence to what was considered normal diplomatic protocol. This too was based on a presumptuous notion; other relations were necessary to have and keep peace and security in the land.

It should be asked what was so tempting about other gods? Well, up until the Israelites went into the Promised Land, their god, Yahweh, was only known as a god of nomads and slaves. He was not a god of landlords. What did He know about planting seed, hoeing, weeding, or harvesting? What does a masonry god know about raising livestock? Even more worrisome, Yahweh had never been a city god. What would he know about administrating and governing a society that wasn't transient? You see, it wasn't that the Israelites didn't like Yahweh or think he wasn't great as a deliverer; He was just insufficient for the task of *thriving* in the land. The sense of divine insufficiency is what drives the need for multiple loyalties. Nobody in the ancient world believed one god could take care of everything. This is why you need lots of them; there are different kinds for different tasks. It is necessary to cover all the bases. It wasn't that the Israelites denied their God or even delegated Him to a lesser place among the gods. It was just hard to believe that through only one god, they could have the blessing of life. Yahweh alone wasn't enough to thrive. The Israelites are enjoined to *stop having*. It is more like God's statement – **you don't need the other gods! I'm enough, really. Trust me in this.** Out of one God, all can be blessed. In a similar way God says, "You don't need what your neighbor has. What I have given you is enough." *Make* blessing don't *take* blessing.

Both the first and the tenth Word call for particular relational distinctions and priorities to be maintained and not blurred. What is behind both of these is the notion that critical social contracts necessary for survival are not a matter of right as much as gift. You shall only have one binding and ruling social reality – Yahweh's presence. The Israelites were to properly maintain the presence of both one god and neighbor. They needed to understand and practice on a fundamental level that having one god as the sole and supreme subject of devotion automatically provides focus and direction to thriving in the world. Something is importantly implied in both of these commands; be satisfied and content with what was given you and in the inheritance he provides.

God's agenda for his people and the world, expressed in the Ten Words, is sandwiched in on both sides with a clarion call.

Don't be restless.
Don't be anxious.
Don't worry and live in fear.
Your God is enough, and your stuff is enough.

Shabbat – Prescription for a Well-balanced Life

Don't take on competing loyalties that will only lead,
to the driven and nagging lie:
to stop is to die, to stop is to die.

Above all, The first and the last Word remind us that in order to have times of rest, our whole life must be orientated to the One who gives it and does it best. God's Shabbat is not isolated, but rather it has a context. God's rest only works within a context where the God of life is given complete and sovereign rule.

Prohibitions Against False Representation

Do not make for yourself false images. Do not worship and serve them.
Do not present a false impression of your neighbor.

The second Word is concerned with "graven images". It is here that the language of image is encountered, only now in a negative sense. *Don't make for yourself carved images.* The verb – make – is the same one used in creation. It is clearly a doing, working activity. Idols put us to work. Making idols goes beyond the work of living. Here again is perhaps a reason why we may not experience rest. Our spare time is used up making, worshipping and serving images. As in the first Word, the phrase "*for yourself*" is in the statement. Carved images were often associated with personalized gods, token gods that could be put in a garment or bag. Having personal idols was a popular practice for the purpose of securing individual attention from the gods. In our world of ever increasing monolithic structures, we are being driven to *carve out* a nitch for ourselves, to somehow mark out ourselves from the depersonalized, faceless crowd of numbers and machines. We'll even carve images on our skin. We desperately need some image of ourselves, or our world, to guide us and give us meaning.

The Hebrew word for image literally is *"a carved thing"*. What really is at issue here is not image verses no image, but false image verses true image. It is between the genuine and cheap imitations, between the original and a copy. The Genesis account clearly lays out a positive view of image. There are some distinct differences between image used in this prohibition and that of the creation account. One noticeable difference is the word for *likeness*. In the Decalogue the *likeness* of idols is **timunah**, it literally means split off. We find **timunah** in the Genesis account in reference to living things being split up into various kinds. It carries the idea of imitation in that it is split off from the real thing or the source. This kind of image does not carry the same clarity as the original. Job 4:15 gives a good picture of this kind of image; it is ghostlike, shadowy, indistinct. The word for *image* of God in man is **cadmut.** It is derivative from the word for blood – **dom.** The god-bearing image in man is of the same blood type. Notice that *image* in idols is one of a copy, while the god-bearing image is related to life. My children bear the image of my wife and I because they are of our blood. Of course, we moderns know that this is really about DNA codes and all that, but the ancients only knew that the life is in the blood. The second word is a prohibition against creating cheap imitations of life rather than producing life.

Idol production is consumptive. It certainly adds to the workload. It consumes more than time and energy though. Ultimately, it consumes us. We become more occupied with making our images come alive than making God's creation thrive. It puts humankind into a frame of thinking in which we presume our task is to re-create everything. We think we have to manufacture life rather than produce it or fill it out. Idol production says creation is unfinished; get to work. Shabbat says creation is perfectly complete; stop working and be blessed. Thrive don't strive. The second prohibition - no graven images- reminds us that there is a huge difference here between loving God and hating him. Notice again, that the Israelites are asked to *stop doing* something. Stop image production.

The ninth word takes on a similar concern about fabricating an impression of another. The injunction seeks to prohibit the community members from responding to a neighbor by being a "worthless witness". The Word prohibits the adherence to the ready temptation to seek the destruction of another by way of false accusation. It prohibits the act of creating a false impression of another that would bring him down or destroy him. It was an insidious form of retribution.

It is easy for us who live in a modern and complex society to underestimate a system of justice that relies heavily on the integrity of witness. Any society, even today, that does not have modern forensics or a good police force places an awesome power into the hands of those who can verify the truth of a matter. A false witness can have a horrific effect on a community. In the case of the Salem witch trials, a mere pointing of the finger meant not only certain condemnation for the accused, but it also spread an atmosphere of suspicion and fear that nearly chocked the life out of all involved. From our perspective today, it turned justice on its heels and made those responsible for justice seem most evil.

It must be understood that a witness in the ancient world had a much broader function than for us today. To bear witness was a solemn responsibility and was the binding force in maintaining the well-being of the society. A witness functioned as a judge, a jury, and a prosecuting attorney. To bear witness is to solemnly warn, encourage, admonish, exhort, charge, enjoin, invoke. Indeed the Ten Words are called "the tablet of the Testimony". Most of all, to bear witness is considered a divine charge and solemn

Shabbat – Prescription for a Well-balanced Life

responsibility to verify the covenant by living by its truth. In this regard, all of Israel was considered a witness.

Although we have an elaborate judicial system, we are not far removed from this. Accusation is still a powerful force in our society. Even if there are no legal proceedings that ever take place, a person can be taken down or cut off (as the Bible calls it) by the insidious power of a fabricated picture of another person. We are an image-obsessed culture and in this market driven economy it is as a Canon commercial said it, "Image is everything." We, and especially our children, are powerfully influenced by the images we are barraged with. It is not just advertisement and tabloids that are to blame though. The infectious and destructive power of presenting false impressions of others begins in those little circles of gossip cloaked under that vain guise of being concerned.

There is a very close connection and powerful link between false images of gods and the way we choose to portray others and ourselves. Both the second and the ninth Word dare us to live in the Creator's world with a true estimation of who God is as well as us. They challenge us to thrive in a world of reception rather than deception. Be reminded though, that image is not abandoned. Truly we are creatures of a visible world. No, the call is to abandon cheap imitations, empty, worthless, vain and lying images.
False imagery, whether of God, our neighbors, or ourselves, has an ironic twist to it. It is motivated by a sense of insufficiency all the while severely limiting our ability to see the bigger picture. As bright and as clear as our new TVs promote themselves to be, they only cloud and distort our picture of who God is and a true sense of who we are. In the second and ninth Word we are admonished to rid our lives of false images. They are contrary to God's rest. False images are endless, restless, demanding, anxious, and most of all destructive. They demand constant attention and can only take life away rather than promote it.

Prohibition Against Self-serving Manipulation
Do not use the Lord's name for worthless purposes.
Do not steal, commit adultery or murder.

The third prohibition can be unfortunately and easily misunderstood. It has been reduced to an injunction against using God's name as an interjection. Although there is a slight connection, this strays from the central concern of the prohibition. The Hebrew verb is nowhere used in reference to speech. It means to bear up, carry, take or lift up. It is best understood with the word it is in parallel with – *shav*, vain, worthless, empty. Don't take up God's name for some worthless end. Don't invoke God's name as some kind of official endorsement of your own agenda. Don't get God's agenda, the Ten Words, mixed up with your own.

This too, is a prohibition against a kind of idolatry. Almost any archeological dig in the Middle East will uncover a pit with a pile of broken potshards in it. If one didn't like the way things were going, one could write a curse on a pot and throw it into a pit while invoking a god's name to put it into effect. The idea was that the person or situation one was displeased with would be broken to pieces in a similar way as the pot. Although the gods were demanding, they could be employed under certain circumstances. They could be useful for personal gain. Invoking a god's name to some purpose was a contractual affair that usually involved some kind of trickery. No god, you see, would willingly help a human thrive without some kind of pay back.

Something of this concern is expressed in the conversation Moses has with God at the burning bush. Moses insists that he can't do anything without having God's name. He would not be empowered without it. God's response is effectually, "Never mind what my name is. I will be, who I will be." I climbed many mountains in Colorado. Most of them were named after the person who first found it or climbed it. I don't know if people got tired of the whole naming thing, but some peaks are named "No Name" peak. God's name is essentially "No Name". Naming things was more than a symbolic gesture of ownership; it was considered to have effectual power to claim possession or rule over. Hence, Adam was to name the animals. Naming is an extension and function of blessing, empowering to thrive. YHWH will in no way be owned by his people or another god; on the contrary, He is the one claiming ownership.

The third Word is a prohibition against claiming that a human agenda has divine sanction. As Brueggemann demonstrates in his book Israel's Praise, ideology is a sort of inside out idolatry.[14] It has to do with the chosen or separated ones taking on a different role other than being the source and dispenser of blessing. Instead, they take on a posture of shear presumption blurring personal desires and Yahweh's. This is the sin that ruined the leaders of Israel. Moses, Saul, David, Solomon, and Jeroboam all succumbed to this.

The third word aggressively addresses the temptation to cloak greedy and self-serving agendas in the guise of a noble or higher cause. It goes back to

---

[14] "The title of this book, *Israel's Praise: Doxology against Idolatry and Ideology*, reflects the way I have shaped the argument…In chapters 3 and 4, I have considered how the proposed world of Yahwistic faith, marked by righteousness, equity, and truth, becomes skewed by royal management. The Psalms then are distorted to symbolize a god (idol) who cannot act, and a social system (ideology) that cannot change or be criticized. Walter Brueggemann, *Israel's Praise,* pgxi. Fortress Press 1989.

the first and most common response to our sin: self-justification. Well does the proverb put it – the road to hell is paved with good intentions (or seemingly good ones). Be reminded that the original sin was an act of taking what was not theirs to have. The first response of the offender was to smooth the offense over with a deified endorsement. There is nothing more hideous than for someone, whether individually or a group, to engage in some outrageous violation against another and then to put God's stamp of approval on it.

The Words: do not kill, do not commit adultery and do not steal, follow suit with the third Word. All three deal specifically with the vital social elements needed for all to thrive in the land. These words seek to put a stop to the practice of taking what another needs for life, all in the name of some better or higher purpose being served. If the third Word gets at the justification for misusing others, the sixth, seventh, and eighth Words get at the means to do it.

All three deal specifically with a kind of anti-socialism, which in our individualistic society is a ready temptation. I am reminded of a passage from Wendell Berry's book <u>Remembering</u>. A journalist asks an old Amish farmer why he doesn't acquire more land to farm. His answer is short but swollen with wisdom. "I'd lose my neighbor."[15] This, I contend, is precisely the condition of most of us. Although we live close to others and with more of them, we have few neighbors. If these violations are put into practice, they essentially eliminate a neighbor by ignoring him, acquiring him or having control over his life. They no longer become neighbors, but disposable employees or property. We unwittingly or not, conscript them into serving a personalized agenda. If we take away the neighbor's ability to thrive, then we lose neighbors. We have no community. Certainly to kill a neighbor whether intentionally or accidentally is a sure way to gain an upper hand over one's neighbor. Committing adultery is like a covert operation, sabotaging the internal fabric of the neighbor's household. It is a direct attack on the command to "be fruitful". The primary concern of the prohibition on stealing has more to do with stealing people; it was a form of kidnapping.[16] Kidnapping had its monetary reward but not from a ransom. No, kidnapped persons became conscripted labor, in other words, slaves or cheap labor. Perhaps these Words seem remote to most of us, until we realize that what is behind all of these is a view of those around us as simply vehicles for our own fulfillment and well-being. When our only view of others is what can be personally gained from the relationship, then we become precariously open to one of these prohibitions. On top of that, and more importantly, we have lost an opportunity to share life with another.

---

[15] Wendell Berry, *Remembering,* pg 85, North Point Press 1995

[16] Gerhard Von Rad, *Deuteronomy, Old Testament Library,* pg59, Westminster Press, 1975

The third Word and its correlatives focus more attention on one of our greatest human weaknesses. We have all kinds of elaborate ways and means to put me first all the while cloaking these intentions from God and neighbor. When we operate like this, we unknowingly create a very uneasy atmosphere. We stir up restlessness rather than promote rest. It is hard for us to realize that the best way to promote our own well-being is to promote the well-being of all.

Shabbat, Something to Hold on To

The Words address Israel's relationship to their god and to the community gathered around Him. They specifically undermine the popular notions of what a relationship with God and neighbor should look like. They all call for something to stop being done. What was so tempting about idolatry? What is so irresistible about the gods? I'll presume to answer an unanswerable question. There is a fundamental human need in all of this. Regardless of how big or small a god is, they must have some visible, tangible, and real to life presence in our physical existence. We can't deal with invisible powers. Spirituality must have some real life correspondence. It's not that it is simply no use to us; even more so, we can't deal with it. It's too much. If we are to be in relationship with a god we need something to hold on to. Divine presence needs to be real to life. This goes back to the question about chaos addressed in the creation account. We also, like the ancients, need to know what ultimately drives the world we live in. Is it chaos or guided presence?

Precisely! Real life is what YHWH is all about. Remember this god of creation is concerned about living things – souls. This is where Shabbat comes in. Our God is not negating this base human need in these prohibitions. The Words against idolatry and wrong-headed human relationships all the more affirm God's concern towards this need. Hold on to what is really real, what is truly life-giving. Shabbat is where you can really embrace the life-giving presence of your God. In the Words of the Decalogue, God separated himself and his people, not for smug competition in the world, but in order that through them, blessing would happen. Out of one, the many are blessed. Rather than working for the gods or having the gods work for you, take a day off. God's real presence among his people is in a work stoppage, in ceasing. It is in life not strife.

In order to keep and to make holy the Shabbat, stop what you normally do for a living and remember.
Honor your father and mother.

The Word on Shabbat is God's answer to self-serving and self-promoting relationships. Oddly, the notion of having a Shabbat is already presumed.

Shabbat – Prescription for a Well-balanced Life

The Shabbat Word is providing instruction on how to keep it rather than on whether to keep it. In other words, there are two things that must be done in order that it be properly observed and made special. So, here it is, God's most direct word on acquiring rest: work for six days, and then stop working and remember.

Interesting enough, God commands that work be done for six days. Perhaps the temptation was as ready to the Israelites as for us: that is to extend the work stoppage to other days. I am reminded of a time when I was riding a bus into downtown. Two men greeted each other and begin talking. At one point, the question was asked, "So, what are you doing?" The other replied, "Oh, I'm out looking for a job," there was a pause and then he continued, "and hoping I don't find one." Probably in the hearts of most of us is a similar desire to increase the proportion of leisure to work. This, however, would lend itself towards exploitation of others to make it happen. God commands all to work, and all to stop working on Shabbat. As Amos and other prophets loudly protested, the tendency became one where those with the means kept others working perpetually in order to have more leisure themselves.[17] This is contra-Sabbath thinking.

God is quite confident that six days is enough time to labor and do all your work. He commands that we do so. The Hebrew word for work is **_melacah_**, and it specifically is applied to one's occupation, what is done for a living, business, or livelihood. It may also apply to the end result of one's work, i.e. workmanship. On Shabbat, the Israelites were to stop their normal work or what they're working on. This is the word used when it says at the end of Genesis 1 that God finished his work. God's business is creating, and this is precisely what he finished doing on the seventh day when he stopped working. There is no need for much word study when it comes to the word Shabbat; it simply means stop, cease, desist, cut off, shut down the busy – ness. Stop working!

Shabbat, however, is a radical break with the way things are. The gods are open 24 hours a day and need constant attention lest your crops fail, your herd is attacked, your computer crash or your stocks lose points. Shabbat is a daring restatement of the way things really are. As I stated earlier, the day God finished creation and stopped working is also the day when God's creative activity turned towards mankind and human history. Creativity didn't stop when God stopped working. It just changed directions. Shabbat is day seven of creation but day one of his loving involvement in history.

This is where the second part of the Sabbath Word comes into view. It is a day to stop working and start remembering the way things really are. This is the way things really are: the Creator says creation is finished, all good gifts

---

[17] Amos 4:1-2

have been given, God's face turns toward the human experience and dilemma. This is precisely why God extruded a people for himself out of the land of perpetual work (Egypt). The Israelites are reminded that this was no easy task.[18] God had to strong-arm the other gods to get them; nonetheless, God did it, and Shabbat is to be the memorial of that. The Hebrew word "remember" is *zakar*, and its basic understanding is to call out, name, or mention. Remembering was not for the ancients a matter of bringing up something forgotten. It was to recall or bring to mind in such a way that it affected present feeling, thought, or action. It is to memorialize. It is not only to set up in such a way that it is impossible to forget it; even more so, it becomes a part of the present reality. Every nation today has memorial days. They are times set aside, holy-days, in order to relive a collective identity. One of the prominent features of the Torah is the amount of commands for holidays. The festivals of Israel are extensions of the Sabbath command, and they all have something to do with re-membering oneself to the covenant. In Shabbat, the Israelites were to re-member not re-create.

Because for most of us holidays are merely an occasion to have some fun and barbeque some burgers, we underestimate the critical importance it played in ancient society. Important in this regard was the reference festivals gave to time. The Israelites, of course, had no clocks or watches, but they also didn't have local places of worship. To gather for worship would have been a monumental effort similar to the camp meetings of the American pioneers. The festivals of remembrance not only gave reference to time, but ultimately it gave all the Israelites a reference to reality. It provided a solid sense of place and purpose for each member.

The Word on Shabbat gives a clear purpose for it. It is for rest. The noun form of the Hebrew word for rest is pasture. Of this kind of rest, King David said it best:

> *The Lord is my shepherd;*
> *I lack nothing.*
> *He makes me lie down in green pastures;*
> *He leads me to water in places of repose;*
> *He renews my life.*[19]

This word means precisely what most of us are after when it comes to rest. It is a place of stillness, tranquility, and repose. The idea is to stretch out with no need to immediately recoil in defense. Unfortunately, neither the Psalmist nor we can make this kind of rest happen. It is a mistake to think so. No, it is the Lord who "makes us lie down" and "leads us to places of repose". God must be allowed to guide his people to it. In a sense, we

---

[18] Deuteronomy 5:15
[19] Psalm 23:1-2

Shabbat – Prescription for a Well-balanced Life

cannot simply set out to do rest. Again, the Sabbath Word tells us what our part is: work six days, and then stop what you're working on and remember. The "rest" is up to God.

It is of critical importance to notice to whom Shabbat is especially for. First, foremost, and often overlooked, it is *for the Lord*.[20] If this is the case, it should be assumed that above all, there is a God who loves, requires, and enjoys rest. Also, for this God, rest is not rest unless it is shared. When Papa has His rest, everything is better.

The second group of people who should have rest are the ones not capable of making it happen by their own means: the children, the employees, the strangers and even the beasts of burden. Rest is not just for the executives who can procure the means to stop working; it is more so for the ones who work under them. It is readily apparent that the picture presented in the fourth Word is one of a household; as indeed, a family generates one's livelihood. A southern plantation would be a similar comparison. The emphasis is clearly not that the head of the family take a hiatus while everyone else keeps the plantation operating. No! The boss is responsible to make rest not take rest. The command is not to take Shabbat, but rather to make Shabbat. Herein lies the notion of blessing. The blessed one is to provide blessing. Out of the one, the many are blessed. This idea comes out more vividly in the many commands concerning festivals. The son of the commandment is the one to provide a fellowship meal for all in his house. Even the resident alien is to be included.

We cannot loose sight that the remembering always includes a meal. One of the derivative meanings of *zakar* is a memorial offering. The sacrificial system was primarily to provide shared meals. Most sacrifices were to be offered by the prominent male, the son of the inheritance and then divided up and offered to the children, the slaves, the sojourner, and the poor. This is called the fellowship, thank, or peace offering. All of these lesser members were not immediately the ones God was in covenant with, but they are nonetheless the recipients of the blessing of God's covenant.

The One to Make Shabbat Happen – Honor the covenant couple

---

[20] Von Rad explains that the term *holy for the Lord* is quite formalized and is rich in meaning. Ultimately, any person, day, season, or thing set apart for the Lord is an act of confession. "The inference to be drawn from this way of speaking of it, which is widespread and fixed, is that Israel regarded the cult as the place where pre-eminently it was incumbent upon her to make room for Yawheh's right and for the claim which he made." Von Rad, Old Testament Theology vol. I; pg 241-242 Harper and Row

We need to take notice of who in particular is to obey this command, or for that matter, any commands of the Torah? It is the bar mitzvoth – son of the commandments. It is the male leader of the household, but is it just a male thing? Take a look at the fifth Word. Once again, there is the assumption that the honoring of parents is already happening. I don't think I'm out of line, when I infer that this is a continuation of the Sabbath Word.

The honoring of father and mother is directed at the recipients of Shabbat: the children, the servants, the aliens, and the poor. They are not to be ingrates, but give weight, respect, and honor to the one who has been given the inheritance. They are to humbly receive, not from the male alone, but from the covenant couple. In the union of the two there is the one source of blessing. Together, they are the one (flesh) source of blessing. Be fruitful and multiply. Do not neglect to notice in the patriarch stories how prominent the role of the wives is in the whole blessing mix. In fact the union with the right women becomes the critical piece in whether the promise is going to happen. Out of the blessed union is the source of blessing for many others. They obviously and physically produce offspring and therein fill out the command to be fruitful, but the command extends the blessing of fruitfulness beyond that. It should extend to all those who are subordinate participants in the covenant.

There are two other items to consider which point to the connection the fifth Word has with Shabbat. The first is the affirmation of well-being. In the Shabbat Word, the promise is for rest. To think again about rest we may consider it in comparison to its opposite – unrest. Mention unrest in our day and one will immediately conjure up words like: riot, violence, murder, upheaval, stress, or heightened tension. This is the same for the ancients. Israel, then, is like Israel now, surrounded by enemies. Almost every Psalm, including Psalm 23 has some prayer in it for relief from enemies. I cannot possibly go into all the implications here as it got played out in Israel's history. I just want to point out that the injunction of rest, well-being, goodness, and blessing is firmly to be carried out, even when "my enemies surround me". As the covenant couple makes a Shabbat, and all the inhabitance receive Shabbat, there will be rest in the land and it will be *tov* – good. Herein lies the very nature and purpose of covenant. It is the one thing in the middle that joins polarities. The earth and man are in the middle of creation. The tree of life is in the middle of (in between) the tree of knowledge and the "lusty trees". Israel and her god are in the middle of the nations, and the covenant couple is in the middle of Israel. All this so one day God can say of man as he did of creation; Wow! This is really good.

The second item to notice is the phrase that God has already commanded Shabbat and honoring parents – as the Lord commanded you. When did this happen? Rabbis have gone around the block more than once with this one. My guess is that these notions had a history prior to the exodus and Mt Sinai.

Shabbat – Prescription for a Well-balanced Life

I'm not going to do any defending of this here; it just may be the case though, that the fourth and fifth words were grounded (pun intended) in creation, in the way things really are.

The creative work of God is working its way into the fabric of human history. It is true of God's creative order and his revelatory order. His truth is marching on. As hard as it is to understand, this happens as much in what God is not doing than in what He is doing. What all can be understood in such a phrase; God stopped working? Human history is still moving towards its completion, towards its rest, its Shabbat. God commanded Shabbat for his people to remind them of what was, and is and is to come. Shabbat is a perfect proclamation of who owns the place. In ceasing, God and creation come together, God's people come together, husband and wife come together, and finally God and humankind come together.

There are days
when we seek things for ourselves and measure failure by what we do not gain.

On the Sabbath,
we seek not to acquire but to share.

There are days
when we exploit nature as if it were a horn of plenty that can never be exhausted.

On Sabbath
we stand in wonder before the mystery of creation.

There are days
when we act as if we cared nothing for the rights of others.

On the Sabbath
we are reminded that justice is our duty and a better world our goal.

Therefore we welcome Shabbat

day of rest.
day of wonder,
day of peace.[21]

---

[21] *Gates of Prayer,* pg 178; Central Conference of American Rabbis

The Truest Meaning of Rest
Jesus and Shabbat

By the time we turn to the New Testament, Shabbat appears hopelessly tarnished by the perpetual Darth Vaders of religious atomism. Shabbat is anything but restful. It is tempting then, to read the Shabbat controversy in the gospels as something Jesus conveniently abrogated. This, in my opinion, would be an unfortunate mistake. Jesus is insteeped in the history of his people. He sees the *whole* history of Israel, including the Torah, leading to him. Granted, Jesus' posture towards the law appears bi-polar, sometimes upholding it, even in its details, and other times sweepingly disregarding it. Let us, however, embrace the posture that the early church insisted on was that of Jesus himself. He is the fulfillment of the Torah. This is not always an easy resolve to the issue; nonetheless, it must guide us. Jesus ***fills out*** the Torah. He fills in the Torah. In my mind, there is more than a casual connection between the filling out of creation, *blessing*, and the filling out to fullness of God's redemptive work. Jesus came not to abolish the Torah, but to usher in the blessing of it. As this pertains to Shabbat, and its rest, Jesus not only upholds it, but he restores it and fills it out. He doesn't limit Shabbat or annul it; on the contrary, he extends it and insists on it. Jesus is Shabbat. In the same way that he reclaims a polluted Temple, so he does a distorted Shabbat.

What Shabbat Had Come to Mean

I have tried to explore some of the intended meaning of Shabbat as we find it in the Hebrew Scriptures. What is intended though, and what was actually played out can be quite a different story. The history of Israel, as presented in the Bible, does not paint a very nice picture of the nation's ability and willingness to obey the Torah. We find, for example, that Josiah had to reinstitute some of the most basic of decimated traditions, like the Passover. We are told at the end of the Chronicler's history, that the exile of the Israelites in Babylon corresponds in some way to the amount of missed Shabbats. Ezekiel makes it quite clear Shabbat was not honored because of their gross disloyalty to Yahweh and their obsession with idols (Ezekiel 20). With the land, temple and throne of David all decimated, it is easy to see what kind of importance Shabbat took on in the rebuilding years. After all, it was one thing that still could be done in the absence of the other institutions.

The books of Ezra, Nehemiah, Haggai and Malachi remind us how difficult the returned exiles found it to be in the land. There was a half-hearted approach to restoration that many knew was not in line with the kind of gross violation the nation had done to get them into this mess. **Threat** was a key operative word. There was the outward threat that the Israelites would loose their distinctiveness and just blend in with the neighbors. Also, there was an inward threat that the worship of Yahweh would not be taken very seriously. Many knew that there needed to be a full-scale repentance and vitality given to the traditions of their god. Once again, the Israelites are faced with the seeming insufficiency of their god. Both the inward and outward threat touch on the themes presented in Shabbat. How can we maintain our distinctiveness – holiness? How can we thrive in a land now inundated with foreign influence – blessing? Ultimately, it was a question of how could exclusive loyalty to Yahweh be maintained in a now hostile and unsympathetic environment?

This impossible task fell in the hands of Nehemiah. It would be a long time before the national institutions would look like any of its prior glory. Besides the real problem still lay on the more local and individual level. Nehemiah set out on a rigorous restoration agenda that was particularly aimed at the common Israelite. So, he went after a purging of the Levitical priesthood and a ban on mixed marriages. Also, he set down strict guidelines for commerce in order to stem the temptation to disregard the Shabbat. Nehemiah's reforms may appear to us as strict, unforgiving, or exclusive. It was the choice of this leader at a most perilous and difficult time. We should notice that these reforms were especially in response to the threat of outsiders, either by hostility or by syncretism. We should also take note how important the observance of Shabbat would become as a national symbol of solidarity and faithfulness in a world where the usual symbols of temple and kingship were nowhere in sight. As the situation continued through the centuries, it is easy to see how the observance of Shabbat could surpass or at least be equal to the status of the former. Indeed it did.

The foreign threat became no greater than when the Greeks set out their cultural war on the ancient world. Up until then, the Jews in all of the Diaspora had worked out, at minimum, a semi-workable coexistence. During this time the synagogue took shape and the Jews had worked out a way to embrace the presence of their god even in the absence of his house, his king, or his land. This is also when a militant pietism arose in response to the very real threat of the annihilation of the Jewish way of life. Thus the Hasidim were birthed, the precursors to the Pharisees. We cannot forget that by the time we get to Jesus there was already embedded into the Jewish psyche memory of many a man, women, and child who were massacred simply because they refused to resist their enemies on a Shabbat. At this time the meaning of Shabbat was infused with new meaning; courage, unflinching loyalty, and staunch resistance to foreign influence were all wrapped up in a few key national symbols of independence. Shabbat took on a symbolic

The Truest Meaning of Rest

badge for the struggle for independence similarly to what the Boston tea party was for the American patriots.

It is not that the intended meaning of Shabbat was lost in all this; but it was infused, perhaps even overshadowed, by another meaning. Also, it is not that this infused meaning was widespread; it was, however, influential and a cause of inner national tensions. The struggle of Jewish *independence, identity*, and *solidarity* was coming to a high-pitched crisis in the time of Jesus. This infused meaning does have some connection to the intent in the Decalogue, that of response to foreign gods and a way to live out a loyalty to their god. Yet at the same time, it subtly turned Shabbat on its heals. Instead of rest, Shabbat was now about resistance, instead of ceasing, it was striving. More importantly, instead of *making* Shabbat for the children, servants, poor, and sojourners it became a way to exclude, not only them, but also even other covenant members. Most of all, Shabbat became more a *response to their enemies* than a response to their god.

Showdown on Shabbat

All of the Gospels give an account of Jesus in conflict with a Jewish opposition over the Shabbat. For one, the Shabbat controversy is neither an isolated point of contention nor the pinnacle one. It is among a string of controversies that build on each other. We should also note that although Jesus appeared to be doing things in an unorthodox manner, even deliberately so, he worked well within the whole framework of Jewish life. We also need to be reminded that Jewish life in first century Palestine was anything but uniform. He observed all holy days, asked his adherents to obey Jewish law, and insisted on the authority of Moses. What is interesting about the Gospel's presentation of Jesus' clash with Jewish authorities is how limited the scope was. What is also important is how vehement the opposition was about some key issues. Ultimately, all of the Gospel's present the Sabbath controversy as the straw that broke the camel's back. It is in response to the issue on Shabbat that a vehement opposition to Jesus begins to solidify.

Matthew's gospel shapes the conflict coming to crises most clearly. He sets up a distinct triad of characters leading to a crisis of decision. There is the little group of Jesus' followers on the one hand, the Pharisees on the other, and Jesus in the middle. These groups are characterized so that they can serve Mathew's intent to present the drama of Jesus and Israel. This critical historical drama has been played out several times before in Israel's history. Matthew's inclusion of the Emanuel passage was sure to remind his listeners that throughout Israel's history there had been critical moments of crisis and decision that changed the destiny of the nation. Mathew wants to show that in Jesus the history of Israel and its God had come to its finest hour. The *crowd* is another character in the drama. They are the audience who must weigh the outcome. Which character best represents the *true* Israel?

With his gospel, Matthew also seeks to remind the early church that it was incubated within the nest of an established and unique ethnic group with a profound sense of historical destiny incased in traditions, rituals and values that had endured an agonizing test of time. The cracks of breach over the meaning of that destiny were initially and exclusively a conflict within the world of Judaism. Matthew wants to assure those who believe Jesus that in Him, the pinnacle of historical destiny of Israel had now come. Jesus did not negate the apparatus that had carried the vision for so long. On the contrary, he had completed it, brought it to its fullest expression, its logical purpose. Jesus had brought out the truest meaning of the Torah life.

Shabbat Controversy in Matthew

Matthew's gospel is most squarely shaped around the crisis of Jesus and Israel. Matthew has arranged his gospel in such a way that the crisis comes to a head in the middle, chapter 13. Sound familiar? Before this chapter, Jesus is presented as an open question to the Jewish nation, including its leaders. They weren't necessarily for him or against him. Like most controversial figures of the time, they were sized up for the most part as to whether they would or could advance the national cause. And like his predecessor, John, Jesus was increasing in popularity and seemed to be endorsing nationalistic aspirations. At the start of chapter 13, Jesus is at the height of his popularity. In a series of parables, Jesus then, decisively lays out his claim on Israel and calls on all to decide. "He who hears, let him hear." Immediately after the series of parables on the kingdom, momentum has already begun to shift. Jesus is rejected in his hometown, John the Baptist was beheaded, and there is now a solidified and intensified opposition to Jesus. The Sabbath controversy is presented in Matthew as one of a few issues that were causing the questions about Jesus to intensify.

Mathew frames up the controversy with the Jews most succinctly with one of his favorite words, *scandolon* – scandal. Wonderings about whether Jesus was stretching the boundaries too far first appear in the Gospel from those *inside* his own movement, from John the Baptist. *Are you the one who was to come, or should we expect someone else?*[22] . Like many of Jesus' sayings, at first hearing, it doesn't seem to answer the question. Take note, however, of the answer. *Blessed is the man who is not scandalized on my account.*[23] The Greek word - **scandalizo** – means to cause to trip up, stubble, ensnare or offend. Jesus understands that he is a cause for people to be tripped up. As with the issue of both the Temple and Roman tax, so it is here. Even though

---

[22] Matt. 11:3
[23] Matt. 11:6

The Truest Meaning of Rest

Jesus knows he is causing a scandal, he communicates that he is not deliberately doing so. His instruction toward taxes indicates this most clearly; essentially he communicates that paying taxes is no big deal and it shouldn't be used as a way to deliberately provoke someone.[24] His instruction towards people whom he healed also indicates Jesus' position that he was not *deliberately* stirring up controversy, even though he concedes that it is happening. He consistently tells the healed ones to go to the priests in compliance with the Torah and not to go around making a public spectacle of it. Most of them did not do as he asked.

In Jesus' answer to John, he points to the things that are the stumbling blocks. People are being healed, and the poor are hearing good news.[25] It is here where, in my opinion, many have missed a critical point in the Gospel's presentation of the healing miracles of Jesus. Simply put, the healing miracles were signs of God's judgment on Israel. Before I go into explaining this, let me make a corrective point about the judgment of God. It is fair to say that many associate God's judgment with some kind of angry condemnation, a definitive lock'em up and throw away the key. This is unfortunate, because over and over God's judgmental intervention is presented as a merciful appeal to turn around a wayward people. God's judgment should be understood more as Him *holding back* condemnation and *holding out* for a change of heart, not as a *giving up* on a relationship in order to replace it with a better one. Even more so, judgment is God's *active and intentional intervention* into a degenerative situation.

When we look closely at the healing miracles of Jesus, including demon exorcisms, as they are presented in the Gospels, a few items of interest appear. Although there are sweeping statements made of Jesus' healing activity – *Jesus healed all of them* – there are relatively few that are mentioned in detail. Of the ones told about, they are relatively *the same ones*. From this, it is my conclusion that the particular healing miracles given space in the Gospels are representative and decisive for demonstrating most clearly what Jesus was about. These are the miracles canonically chosen by the early church to best reveal the role they played in the drama of Jesus and Israel. This is precisely how Matthew masterfully shapes the miracle accounts in his Gospel.

Matthew uses the healing accounts most sparingly. They are compacted together in a brief two-chapter run, and strategically placed between the first two major speeches of Jesus.[26] This grouping of miracles is Matthew's first interlude that he places between the five major sermons of Jesus. He does this to help illustrate that Jesus' authority was not only in word but also in

---

[24] Matt. 17:24-27
[25] Matt. 11:4-6
[26] Matt. 8-9

deed. From the start of the Gospel onward, Matthew frames up the question for his audience. Who in Israel's history *really* were the ones who faithfully responded to God's initiative? Were they the leaders of Israel? Or were they, more often than not, harlot mothers, foreigners, outcasts, and prophets?[27] The one's responding to God's initiative are not always the ones who you would readily expect. Matthew wants his readers to think again about that. The healing pericope in Matthew 8-9 illustrates this point. Just as a lowly rural couple from Nazareth, pagan priests, confessing common Jews, and brigand-looking Galilean fishermen embraced and welcomed God's initiative instead of Jerusalem, so are lepers, Roman officers, demoniacs living in graveyards, paralytics, and even the dead. For some, these happenings are good news and welcoming omens; but for others, especially the ones you would think should recognize and welcome them, they are a negative commentary. The healing miracles of Jesus reflect poorly on them. They are *tripping up* the very people that one would think should have a solid handle on this kind of thing. It's like watching a politician who is at a loss of words at a rally. This is odd, out of place? The crowds are saying, "Nothing like this has ever been seen in Israel!" They are filled with awe and praising God who had given such authority to men. But to those who the healings are a negative commentary on, they can only respond negatively.

The healing stories of Jesus very much echo the healing stories in the Hebrew Bible. Several come to mind. One example is when Moses stopped the plague in the wilderness. Elijah raised a widow's son from the dead. Elisha healed the commander of the Aramean army from leprosy. Hezekiah is healed by Isaiah and given an extension on his life. There is something important to notice about these. They occur sparingly *and at times of crisis and conflict within Israel.* They occur in seasons of judgment by God. Finally, read the context of Isaiah 53. Matthew directly references it in regards to the healing miracles of Jesus. It is about being utterly astounded that the very people whom the servant has suffered and endured the hardships of exile with, are the very same ones who are ruthlessly and mercilessly turning on him with blame for their miserable plight. I think I am on firm ground then, to say that the healings in the Bible function ironically as warnings and judgments on an unbelieving people in a time of crisis. But as was already mentioned, they also function as demonstrations of God's power and desire to restore a wayward people. This is behind Jesus' response to the Baptist's wonderings about Jesus. It is important when looking at the Sabbath controversy because it is clearly Jesus' *healing* activity that is both the harbinger and crux of the matter.

This is precisely the meaning Jesus attributes to his miracles. Frustrated by the double-bound thinking many of the Jewish authorities are framing the

---

[27] Matt.1-3

The Truest Meaning of Rest

Baptist movement in, Jesus responds.[28] They ought to have been able to easily interpret the meaning of these events. The healings should have triggered a warning signal to respond now to God's initiative![29] Ominous clouds of judgment were coming and one ought to prepare.[30] As Jesus pointed out, healing rabbis where not out of the ordinary at that time.[31] I hold that the particular healing stories given prominence in the gospels are the ones that echoed most clearly the healing stories of Israel's history. This is what so scandalized the national leaders. Point blank, Jesus' healing activity was the hotbed of contention with Jewish authorities whether it happened on Shabbat or not. Ultimately though, it wasn't Jesus' teaching, preaching or healing that was so problematic. After all, there had been all kinds of rabbinic activity like that. It was the *meaning* that Jesus gave to those words and activities that was the central conflict. This is what is critically addressed in Matthew 11-12. Jesus boldly announces that through him alone the Father's will and activity was being accomplished. Through this One, the many are receiving the blessing of God's kingdom.

The Good News Preached - Shabbat Restored - Matthew 11:25-30

Jesus places the loci of God's initiative in this critical juncture of Israel's history squarely on himself. Jesus' metaphor of choice to defend his activity is the household. Jesus argues the issue over the Sabbath, miracles, and demons under the rubric of head of the household. It is not just any household, but especially the *royal and priestly household* that Jesus calls to mind.[32] The argument is between Jesus and Jewish authorities. What they are vying for is patriarchal rights. Who is the master of the house, the one to call the shots? From this pericope on, and until the climax of Jesus' call to decision in chapter 13, Jesus stakes his claim as having a unique and superior authority over God's household as the firstborn son.

Envisioned in the Decalogue was that the household of the **bar mitzvoth** would be the loci for Shabbat to happen. Out of the one, the whole household, especially those without covenantal rights, would be blessed. Again, the children, the servants, the resident aliens, the poor, the cripple, etc. would especially enjoy a Sabbath rest. The son of the commandment was responsible to *make* a Shabbat, not just to *take* one. This is the image that Jesus defends the gospel with.

---

[28] Matt. 11:7-19
[29] Matt. 11:20-24
[30] The Pharisees believed their agenda of priest-like purity was precisely the formula for preparation.
[31] Matt. 12:27
[32] Matt. 17:25-26

I praise you, Father, Lord of heaven and earth. In a rare designation, *Lord of heaven and earth*, Jesus echoes the Shabbat of Genesis 2. As the Lord of creation had *set apart* the seventh day, so now the Father has *set apart* his only son. The Father has handed the household over to Jesus[33] The blessing of the Shabbat is now being distributed in the itinerary of Jesus to *the little children.*[34] As it was always supposed to be, the head of the household should take great delight in the all-embracing blessing of Shabbat.[35] The realm of God's Shabbat – *all these things* - is now being offered through Jesus.

What may not seem obvious in regards to Shabbat is explicitly brought to the fore in verse 28. *Come to me, all who are weary and burdened and I will give you rest.* It seems like the first five commandments of the Decalogue could be summed up in such a phrase as, *come to me…I will give you rest.* The word for *weary – kopiao-* is one of many words with the prefix **kop.** Such words carry meanings such as: mourning, be cut off or cut down, defeated. Ironically, it can mean to stop or cease in a negative sense, i.e. death. The word for burden is used in the sense of constrained or conscripted labor. This word combination goes beyond merely speaking of the hard work of a job. Jesus understands (because he too lived like that) that many a *covenantal* member had been bound by a situation of perpetual work. For sure, the Jewish nation still had overlords whose gods had no idea about taking a day off. Although there is a negative meaning to Jesus' activity, there is even more so a positive meaning. The day of consolation has arrived in Jesus. God's people who have been under the burden of exile for 400 years are now being comforted. The very heart of a Sabbath rest is coming to fruition in Jesus. The word for rest here, ***anapauo,*** carries meanings such as, *re*fresh, *re*new, *re*store, ***and revive***. All these ideas are included in the notion of Sabbath rest.

The rest of God, even in the Decalogue, still required that something be done. In verse 28, Jesus not only instructs those who want such rest but also gives an important qualifying reason. *Take my yoke upon you and learn from me. Yoke* is, of course, used figuratively. It is the most common expression for the burden of conscripted labor, slavery or for the burden of life's obligations. The Torah was also considered a yoke worthy of carrying. That one should learn of God on Shabbat was well established in Jesus' day. Once again, Jesus is not abrogating the Sabbath command as much as he is saying that he is the perfect Teacher for it, because he is *gentle and humble*.

In this passage, Jesus clearly gives his bent on Sabbath rest. It is in him alone. He invites anyone who is experiencing endless toil, labor, strife, and

---

[33] Matt. 11:27
[34] Matt. 11:5-6
[35] Matt. 11:26

obligation to come to his Sabbath rest. Shabbat does not eliminate any of the above lists. While we take a day off, obligation and work await us and even pile up in our absence. Jesus assures those who take him up on his offer that the burden of his Sabbath rest is *nothing* compared to the burden of perpetual work.

The Burden of Rest

At this point the question seems pressing? How can the notion of *rest* be so closely *tied* to that of a *yoke*? Is not this whole notion of a yoke going against the notion of Shabbat, a ceasing from labor? For the most part, *yoke* conjures up negative images in the Bible. The most prominent one is the Israelites longing to be free from the *yoke* of foreign potentates. It is not the notion of yoke itself that is made out to be a villain, however, for God's rulership is considered a yoke. It is that foreign *yokes* were considered oppressive and unbearable. They offer no relief; even more so, they reverse the role of a blessed one. Instead of being a source of blessing for their subordinates, they demand their subordinates be a blessing to them. Two positive images of *yoke* in the Hebrew Bible may be pertinent here. They associate *yoke* with a source of blessing and of ceasing in the sense of non-resistance.

Genesis 27 presents us with the continued saga of Jacob and Esau's fractured relationship. Remember that the patriarchal stories are greatly concerned about how the blessing, of those chosen by God, will be passed on and how the creative activity of God will be continued in the history of man. As I've mentioned in my commentary on Genesis 1, the one with the blessed endowment is the one bearing the image of the ancestor. Image is a rulership term. It is said of Esau that he was under the yoke of Jacob. This is precisely the case because Jacob is the one with the blessing and the ability to bless. Esau was not denied blessing; it was simply to be had via harnessing up with Jacob. Jacob's yoke was Esau's blessing. All he had to do was to not do something. Don't resist. Sadly, Isaac prophesies that Esau will break off the yoke, and estrange himself from God's blessing.

In Jeremiah, yoke is used, interestingly enough, in an intense symbolic conflict that the prophet has with the false prophets. Jeremiah actually places a yoke on himself and walks through the streets of Jerusalem. The people get the unfavorable point. As Jeremiah says it, "Bow your neck under the yoke of the king of Babylon; serve him and his people, and you will live." Jeremiah instructs the people that it is God's will that they *not resist* the rulership of Babylon. Accompanying this exhortation is the promise of blessing; *you will live.* Jeremiah means this quite literally, yet it echoes the deeper meaning of blessing, to be empowered to thrive. The prophet Hananiah is preaching a contrary message however. He breaks off

Jeremiah's prop and tells the people that God is about to break the *yoke* of foreign rule. To this Jeremiah responds; the yoke of non-resistance to God's judgment is easy, but the yoke of resistance will be harsh. The *yoke* is one of Jeremiah's most important symbols. It is never yoke vs. no yoke, but the yoke of false gods vs. God's yoke, which is the covenant (Jer. 30:8-9). Like Esau before them, however, the inhabitance of Jerusalem resisted God's yoke, with disastrous consequence.

Bob Dylan could sum up well the relationship of yoke to rest. "It may be the Devil, or it may be the Lord; but you're gonna have to seeerve somebodai". Shabbat rest is a simple but hard pill for us to swallow. To cease – in God – is to remind and reinforce that we are not masters of the universe. It is not just a ceasing from work; even more so it is a ceasing of resistance. We are blessed and enter God's Shabbat because we have not seized or acquired blessing ourselves. We do not individually appropriate God's rest. We enter God's rest by being under the blessing of the Blessed One. The One set apart by God for blessing. We find rest, even in the midst of sorrows and strife when we willingly give-in to wearing the yoke of the man of sorrows. This yoke is comfortable and inconsequential.

Davies, in his commentary on Matthew, says, "Mt. 11:25-30 is a capsule summary of the message for the entire gospel."[36] In one fell swoop, Jesus declares that he is the very embodiment of both Wisdom and Torah. The Torah was considered the *yoke* of God which many a teacher would encourage his student to wear; no rabbi ever said however, take on *my yoke*. In this pericope we have the kind of declaration that is similar to Jesus' temple proclamation – *I will raise the temple in three days*. He affirms that in his life, words, and deeds are the full expression of God's will. As Shabbat was central in Moses' Torah, so it is central in the good news of Jesus. *Come to me, put on my yoke, learn of me, and I will grant you rest.* Essentially Jesus declares; *I am Shabbat,* or as Jesus says it, *Lord of Shabbat.* Out of this One, the blessing of the Kingdom is being distributed.

The Lord of Rest – Mt. 12:1-13

The Pharisees went out and plotted how they might kill Jesus. This is the end result of Jesus confrontation with the Pharisees over Shabbat. To repeat what has been said, the real source of contention was not over fine legal points of what constitutes *work* on the Shabbat. The sages had haggled over that one for centuries and it had never constituted killing someone over it. It was not over Shabbat vs. no Shabbat but over the *central meaning* of it. Jesus does more than argue for the meaning of the critical national symbols, he claims to be the very *embodiment of them*. There are three things being presented in

---

[36] W.D. Davies and Dale Allison Jr.: *International Critical Commentary: Matthew* vol.II, pg 296, T & T Clark EdinBurgh 1998

The Truest Meaning of Rest

Matthew's only presentation of the conflict with the Pharisees over Shabbat. First, Jesus calls for a return to its original meaning and intent. Second, Jesus, as he does with almost any Torah issue, advocates an *extension* of the Shabbat as opposed to an interpretation that increasingly limits its scope. Finally and most importantly, Jesus subsumes *the whole history and meaning of Shabbat* in him. Essentially he says, "I am the Shabbat of God."

It is no mistake that Matthew places the Sabbath story right on the heels of Jesus bold summary of his gospel. Matthew deliberately places the statement, *Come to me...I will give you rest*, adjacent to the Sabbath story. This is Matthew's preferred style, proclamation then demonstration, word and deed, sermon then illustration. It is Matthew's way of saying, *the Word became flesh and dwelt among us*. It also mimics the style of Deuteronomy were commands of principle are placed adjacent to practical implications.

The story begins with Jesus and his disciples rummaging through a barley field. There is a simple reason for this; they were hungry. The story calls attention to the fact that Jesus was not eating the grain; only his disciples were. It seems as though Jesus had rather intentionally set up this scenario. Yes, Jesus wants to put an exclamative stamp on his Sabbath proclamation. As with so much of who Jesus was, he acted as if he had lived out the whole history of Israel, from the first day of creation onward. So, it feels here like Jesus is leading his disciples into another historical reverberation. Just as Boaz granted Ruth gratuitous access to his field, so does Jesus with his disciples. In yet another of Jesus audacious maneuvers, he gives appearance *as if it was his field* they were gleaning. This is fitting of a blessed one to offer the bounty of his harvest, especially to the poor.

There are two important associations being made here. First, Jesus is applying the gleaning command found in the Torah. Second, when he does this he identifies his entourage as being among the poor. Nowhere in the Torah is the concern for the poor and alien woven so tightly in with the Shabbat as in Leviticus 19. There it places the gleaning command and the command for the covenant couple to provide a fellowship meal right on the heels of the summary command to be a holy people and keep Shabbat. The concern for the disadvantaged is clear from a reading of Leviticus 19. Verse 15 expresses the concern well; d*o not pervert justice; do not show partiality to the poor or favoritism to the great, but judge your neighbor fairly.* This concern is summed up in verse 18; *love your neighbor as yourself.*

That Jesus would associate his disciples as the poor is important in Matthew's gospel and for this story. Only Matthew adds the gleaning story to the Sabbath controversy over healing. In the gospel, Jesus persists in his picture of those following him. They are the humble, the poor, the little ones, the least of all, the sick, the enslaved, the burdened, the hungry. They are his family. That these are being gathered in should be a sign of great hope. The long awaited kingdom is arriving. In this story, Jesus' disciples are associated with those being rescued and restored.

There was not a Pharisee alive who would object to the gleaning or healing commands. Indeed, they had allowed for the rescue of endangered property even on the Shabbat. Their objection is that gleaning and healing constitutes work and should not be done on Shabbat. No doubt, anyone who would desire to keep Shabbat would have to continuously ask the question of what constitutes work. But as I had discussed in the Genesis passage, everything didn't stop on the Shabbat. Indeed the creative work of God not only continued but is also highlighted on the seventh day. God's creative activity didn't cease on the Shabbat; it changed directions. It is a living sign that God has graciously turned toward mankind. Over the centuries the legitimate concern to protect the Shabbat had slowly choked out the intent and hog-tied its scope. Here Jesus takes prerogative to broaden out the arena of the Shabbat back to its *original intent*. The seventh day should be the day of days to *love your neighbor as yourself*, that all creation finds rest, restoration, and satisfaction. Sabbath rest is found where mercy is given.

Jesus is probably just as concerned as the Pharisees about the critical symbolism that Shabbat was in raising national solidarity. Like the Pharisees, he thinks that Shabbat should be an emancipation proclamation. Both Jesus and the Pharisees believed the Torah to be the yoke of freedom. Jesus understood, against a historical distortion, that being a blessed one should mean restoration for the many. It should proclaim; "let freedom ring out". The vision of Shabbat is that God's holy people would ring out the bell of freedom for all to gather around. Instead, it had turned into a rallying cry of freedom for the few, and exclusion of the many. This was utterly counter to Shabbat, and Jesus emphatically declares: "all goodness is permitted on the Shabbat". Doing good and showing mercy is the creative *work* of the Shabbat. It is the season where we can proclaim that , in God, there is *life without strife*.

Jesus goes beyond promoting the original scope and intent of Shabbat. He goes beyond the arena of a Haggadic rabbi debating Halakic rabbis over legalistic fine points. He claims more than a superior interpretation of how best to implement the Shabbat. He claims that all of this is funneled and filled out in himself and his little group. Out of this One (holy), God's empowering life (bless) is being lavishly poured out. The gospel of Jesus is Shabbat. It is this proclamation that the Jewish authorities rightly determined as a serious and dangerous threat.

Jesus first reminds his accusers that the kings of Israel always had an interpretive prerogative.[37] Even when David was a renegade, he still

---

[37] Matt. 12:3-4

understood his favored status before God. It is no accident that Jesus points to this story in Israel's past. David was God's chosen king even when he looked more like a brigand and fugitive. The comparison with Jesus was apparent. Furthermore, Jesus reminds his opponents that not all work stops on Shabbat. As I've said before, Jesus pronounces; the priests do work on Shabbat. This, however, is not the most important point. What is critical for Jesus is what constitutes Sabbath work. That work is mercy. Shabbat is the covenant between God's creation and mankind. God's gracious turning towards mankind is the creative work of the Shabbat. This is why the priests can *desecrate the day*. Jesus argues that *something greater than* both David and the Temple is among them. All these great national symbols are not now negated but subsumed in Jesus. Jesus is the greatest expression of Shabbat.

Jesus does not stop with his "greater than" statement. In his mercy declaration, he goes on the offensive against his opponents. He aims at what is at the heart of the Pharisaic agenda. It is here where Jesus again addresses the claim of patriarchal rights over the household. In Jesus' translation of Israel's most famous prophetic quote he counters the scribal claim that the prophets were the Pharisee's predecessors. All rabbinic authority to interpret the Torah was based on this claim. Jesus now claims to posses sole prophetic authority.

To obey is better than sacrifice. These words are first found on the lips of Samuel.[38] The story is well known, for it was the breaking point with Israel and its first king. Saul had failed to obey the prophet's word. He saved *for himself* what should have been dedicated to the Lord. Saul defends his actions by claiming that the spoils from battle were preserved in order to offer them as sacrifices to the Lord. Samuel negates that assumption. He boldly claims that it was a rebellious and arrogant act equal to divination and idolatry. For Samuel, Saul proved that he had not listened to God's voice; he had rejected the word of the Lord. Saul declares that attentive listening to God's word is better than ritualistic performance.

Ritual is an essential social element, but in this case, God explicitly did not ask for that. Even more important, God insists that social rituals be instilled with meaning and heartfelt devotion. Samuel's saying became the rallying cry of the great prophetic movement of the 8th and 7th centuries B.C. At that time, both Israel and Judah had become rich and prosperous nations. Celebrations became lavish displays of extravagance rather than humble renewals of the covenant.[39] The extravagance should have spilled out in blessing for the less prosperous. Instead, it had a hoarding effect. The riches were gained by, as Amos puts it, "trampling the poor"[40]. All the prophets of

---

[38] I Sam. 15:22-23
[39] See Amos chapters 4-5
[40] Amos 5:11

this time: Amos, Isaiah, Hosea, and Micah, aggressively go after this abuse of Israel's worship. Especially targeted are the *blessed ones* who ought to be blessing others. They were obfuscating their chosen status for the purpose of self-fulfillment. Blessing is so the earth can be filled, not the self. When this gets flipped over, God proclaims; *I despise your Shabbats, I cannot bear your evil assemblies...Stop doing wrong, learn to do right.*[41] *Let justice roll on like a river, righteousness like a never-failing stream.*[42] *He has shown you oh man, what is good and what the Lord requires of you, but to do justly, and to love mercy, and to walk humbly with your God.*[43] **I desire mercy and not sacrifice.**[44]

It is apparently this verse from Hosea that Jesus directly quotes.[45] But let us not limit it to that, for it is a whole prophetic tradition that is wrapped up in this slogan. It is in this verse that Jesus steals the very thunder of the Pharisees. Jesus claims he posses what the Pharisees and especially the scribes, who were mostly Pharisees, claim they posses: the Spirit of the prophets, spiritual authority, and the keys of the kingdom.

The Hebrew word for *mercy* in the Hosea verse is **chesed**. It means kindness, but it has a spreading array of meaning. Most likely here, it carries the meaning of devoted affection. It means the kind of tender affectionate display that people who love each other offer. It is tender devotion. Unfortunately, as the harshness of an exilic life went on through the centuries, the tender part got lost. In its place came an increasing notion of *zealous* devotion. **Chesed** becomes the choice word for pious display. In the two centuries before Christ it became the slogan of a sometimes militant Jewish resistance movement known as the **Chasedim,** from the word **chesed.** In a charged statement, Jesus ironically tells the "pious ones" to go back to the books and learn what piety means. He effectively tells them that they don't know the meaning of the word. How can this be compared? It is like telling the Pope to go and find out what *Vicar of Christ* means. Say what?

Jesus is fighting for more than an exegetical preference over the meaning of a word. He is fighting for the heart of Israel. The Greek word for mercy here is **eleos.** It overlaps the meaning of **chesed.** It means kindness, mercy, compassion, and even clemency. Mose Alison, a jazz singer, has a song in which he sings, "Everybody is crying for mercy...when they don't know the meaning of the word".[46] Jesus is saying the same. More importantly, Jesus is saying he is the meaning of it. Listening response to God should always lead

---

[41] Isa. 1:12ff
[42] Amos 5:24
[43] Micah 6:6-8
[44] Hosea 6:6
[45] Matt. 12:7
[46] Mose Allison, *Everybody's Cryin' Mercy,* Audre Mae Music - BMI

one to loving kindness towards all, a tender hearted devotion towards God in which one senses his blessed state before his God and wants to share blessing with others. Jesus' gospel is the Chesed of God towards us. It is an emancipation declaration. It is the hearts cry of Shabbat! Amen!

It is Finished

Let us not talk down on the Pharisees. They were so close. It is precisely this reason that the gospels devote most of their "Jewish-Christian" dialogue to them. It is precisely why the exchange was so heated. They both knew they were vying for the heart of Israel, for the future of God's people. Why can't we see in this Jesus' desperate attempt to win his opponents rather than to condemn them? They knew Shabbat was central to God's will. They knew God wanted all-out devotion. They knew God wanted to unite his people under one banner so that they could be the blessing for the world. Somehow, something got lost in all that, but Jesus was offering it to all of Israel in the proclamation of his gospel.

It was one of the most disturbing questions of the apostolic Church. How could it be that the very people who should have embraced Jesus the most are the ones who violently opposed him? This pressing question was the driving force for Matthew's Gospel. Contrary to the way many have read this gospel, Matthew is *not* trying to prove that God *rejected* his people and went out to get a *new* people. At least in this gospel, Matthew has carefully distanced *the crowd* from the only other progressive Jewish movement with a potential for survival post Temple, rabbinic Judaism. Jesus did not reject God's people, but he did claim to be the rightful and superior heir of spiritual authority for that people. He does not claim this authority by circumventing Moses. Instead, he insisted Moses would have easily subordinated his Torah to the gospel. Both the Pharisaic and Baptist movements knew that Israel must be reconstituted in some way or it would be annihilated. It then became a question of who would have authority over God's house? Who had a better claim to having the yoke of God's Torah? Who has God's blessing on them? Who would be the source of blessing?

The last words of Jesus on the cross are, *it is finished.* Does Jesus echo the declaration of Genesis 2:1? On the seventh day, God's work in creation was completed. It was the finished work that constituted a ceasing time. The failure of the Jewish leaders to recognize the Blessed One did not thwart God's long drive from primeval history to the this pinnacle crisis in Israel's history. Even in the horrors of the cross, God's gracious turning towards his people and mankind was being completed. From this point on, God's great Shabbat over mankind's history would be instituted. On that day, God rested from his striving with mankind. On that day, restoration was realized. God made that day holy, by the death of his only Son, and on resurrection

Sunday, God blessed the dawning of an eternal rest where God would be all in all. Out of this Crucified One, the blessing of the kingdom came.

And Jesus came and spoke to them, saying, "All power is given unto me in heaven and in earth."
(Out of the One)
  Go therefore, and teach all nations, baptizing them in the name of the Father, and of the Son, and of the Holy Ghost:
  Teaching them to observe all things whatsoever I have commanded you: and, lo, I am with you always, even unto the end of the world. Amen.
(The many are blessed)

A Sabbath Prayer
Another week of work is ended;
Again Shabbat brings welcome peace.

We pause from our labors
To let Shabbat give another dimension to our lives.

These Sabbath candles are symbols,
Of the holiness we seek.

Their brightness dispels gloom
And lights a path to faith and hope.

Their glow reminds us of the sacred bonds
That link us to our people
Over space and time.

Their radiance summons us
To fulfill our people's mission

To cast the light of freedom, justice, and peace
Upon all the world.[47]

---

[47] *Gates of Prayer,* Central Conference of American Rabbis, pg. 219

GOD'S RESTLESS REST
Hebrews 2-5[48]

Introduction – The Rest of Inconvenience

A wagon train is creeping its way across the plains of Colorado. Timing is of the essence. They are trying to make it to the gold fields of California and over the Sierras before winter sets in. The promise of riches awaits them, but lethal tragedy is their unwelcome travel companion. Should they forgo traveling on the Sabbath? Doesn't the whole notion of stopping in this circumstance seem ridiculous?

A Jewish family in Warsaw has been rounded up and quarantined in a rundown part of the city. German soldiers have cut off most of their ability to survive. Conditions are getting worse and then there are rumors that the people taken from the ghetto are being killed. In the midst of the squalor and terrible uncertainty a family gathers in a musty cellar. They light the Sabbath candles and begin their celebration of God's holy day.

Is Sabbath rest a bunch of flowery talk? What about Shabbat in hard times? Is Shabbat more for the prosperous and the well off? In the face of many of life's struggles, can one afford to take a break? It is all well and good for those who have nice homes, good secure jobs or careers, and healthy families, but can someone who is faced with severe hardship, disaster, threat, or want even think in such platitudes? Isn't Shabbat more for the settled and secure than for those who are facing uncertainty and transience?

Admittedly, the notion of a time to stop and repose in many circumstances seems farfetched, stupid, or even dangerous. How could a homeless person or a family that has been forced to flee their life and home because of economic or violent distress even think of rest? What would my friend in Monrovia think of repose right now? The city is once again in the throws of civil war. He struggles daily to find safe drinking water. His family huddles together at night under the crack of gunfire and threat of random and ruthless violence.

---

[48] As with the other chapters, it would be good to become familiar with Hebrews 2-5 in conjunction with this chapter.

These are indeed the more severe examples, but what about milder forms of restlessness or unsettlement? Does one think of rest in that anxious abyss of unemployment? Wouldn't a family being torn apart by divorce find the notion of Shabbat almost laughable? How does one experience rest in God in the midst of a church scandal or split? There are even milder forms of uneasiness that seem to challenge Shabbat: a loss of purpose or the exhausting monotony of a stressful and routine job amidst the never-ending stream of unpaid bills.

As much as I've insisted that Shabbat is a response to God and not an opportunity to pick a fight with the world, it must be admitted that Sabbath rest has its adversaries. In the scenarios envisioned above, Shabbat seems to fly in the face of the very notion of survival. It seems like a mere pipedream to many facing dire situations or a most uncertain condition. Admittedly, one is compelled to wonder just how doable or even reasonable Shabbat is. As dreamy nice as Sabbath rest sounds, does it ever really match reality?

The early church was of course familiar with hardship, and they dealt with the questions posed above. They too faced the normal trials and struggles of survival. On top of that, however, the small Jewish sect began to confront the meaning and reality of the Jesus event more and more. Jesus had radically transformed the meaning and essence of Jewishness and their religious traditions. They were thrust, unwillingly, into an intense and often vicious struggle for their own survival as well as for the heart and soul of Israel. They found many of their traditional social moorings being pulled out from under them. The people who they thought were in the struggle with them turned out to be their most ardent opponents. They were increasingly marginalized and even criminalized by their own people. Ultimately, they became an 'unsanctioned' religion and an enemy of the state. Their adherence to Jesus had landed them in a restless, anxious, and frightening place. They too had to ask whether rest was doable in such circumstances.

It is interesting how uncontroversial the Shabbat is in the New Testament. Apart from the gospel accounts it is hardly mentioned. With all the intense issues about "the law" in the early church, one might think that the Shabbat would have been central. Significant in this regard is its absence from the list the first Council gave to the Gentile Christians specifically concerning issues of "the law". Paul does mention it in a corrective. Following Jesus' example, Paul doesn't renounce the Shabbat or keeping holy day; instead, he redirects the emphasis away from making those things a source of contention.

There is a reasonable explanation for the absence of controversy over the Shabbat in the early church. The first Christian community kept it. There was nothing to discuss. Furthermore, and especially because of their Lord's words on the subject, the early Christians had probably put aside issues around what constitutes work and laid the emphasis where Jesus did: that is, what constitutes rest. To hear the stories of Jesus told by the apostles, to share around the table, and to marvel at the glorious works of God in Christ were rest indeed. The early Church was thoroughly consistent with what Jesus taught about Sabbath rest. Sabbath rest is best found in the One who is the Master Sabbath maker and keeper.

Profoundly then, Shabbat sets before the believer and the believing community a moving target and a crucible of choice. Is it counter to reality or is it its most crucial element? Must one work for rest? This choice held as true for the early church as it does for us.

As the last major passage in the Bible on Sabbath rest is examined in the book of Hebrews, most of the themes already discussed will be reiterated as well as taken to new depths and heights. The language of rest continues: image, day, cease, and completion. Shabbat was not abrogated by the early church but profoundly embraced. As since the beginning, God's Sabbath rest is only experienced in the middle of life, as any of us know it to be, not on its periphery.

With so many things related to Jesus, so it is with Shabbat. Polarities come together into one; tensions are not resolved but mysteriously held together without destroying one or the other. This is so much the case in the Hebrews pericope that outwardly it appears (only to those without faith, as the author insists) as irony, paradox, or blatant contradiction. In this regard, there is an apparent doubletalk when it comes to God's rest, for it talks in terms of a restless rest, transient settlement, guarded vulnerability, moving target, unfinished business, and of being a katapausiphobiac[49] – one who fears the lack of rest. Sabbath rest must be wrested from our lives.

The author of Hebrews must persuade his listeners that they are in a wilderness of indecision. As the early church began to discover more and more just what a profound event happened in Jesus, some of the Jewish adherents began to back away from the implications. This had caused their faith to freeze up. It is as my friend calls it: "option lock". They found themselves in the wandering desolate no man's land of indecision. This, the author insists, is the worst kind of restlessness and is not in keeping with following Jesus regardless of the circumstances.

There is a restlessness that is synonymous with aimlessness: that is wandering. Transience is not always the fault of the wanderer. After all, Abraham and his sons were semi-nomads. Circumstances can often

---

[49] I have made up this word by combining the Greek word for rest – *katapaus* – and the one for fear – *phobos*.

overwhelm the best-laid plans. There is, however, a wandering that is self-induced, and it has a lot to do with indecisiveness. Having more than one goal or destination set before a person in turn brings this about. Most of us have had times in our life where we had choices before us that we knew would determine much about the way the rest of our life would take shape. That time of indecision is a wilderness, a parched land of scarcity, and a restless, anxious, sleepless place. Most of the time, we make a decision and go with it. Then, things settle back down. If we choose not to choose, and stay in the limbo land of indecision, then we suffer an intensified restlessness. Rest is found in Jesus. It is not only found in who he was as an historical figure, but in whom he was in eternity's past and whom he has become. To embrace that fully – that is to follow through with the full implications and ramifications of whom Jesus is- is Shabbat.

Wilderness of Indecisions – The Crisis of the Church in Hebrews

Although there is a broad range of ideas concerning the details of the church situation in the book of Hebrews, there are some things that can be picked up about where this particular group of Christians found themselves.

They were Jewish Christians. As did the church in Acts, they started out their embrace of Jesus within the full context of the Jewish culture, religion, and political spectrum. They supported the Temple and the Torah. They attended a local synagogue. More than likely, they were very devote and zealous of their faith, which was what lead them to taking Jesus seriously in the first place. They may not have been associated with the Pharisees, which was a progressive Jewish movement, but with more conservative and sectarian minded Jewish groups active at the time. These groups, like disciples of John the Baptist and the Essenes, held an intense interest in the Temple and the priesthood. They tended to view the corruption of the Temple and priesthood in more stark terms and advocated a more radical purification and reform of it. Nevertheless, they still gave a central place to these critical Jewish institutions.

It can be deduced from a reading of Hebrews that this church was facing troubled times. The author makes it clear that it was not a severe persecution that would lead to martyrdom; even so, it is apparent that they were facing an opposition of some kind severe enough to warrant the loss of their property and social position. Apparently they were willing to help other believers who faced hardship because of their embrace of Jesus, but became severely rattled when the winds of opposition turned on them. They found themselves embroiled in the intensified Jewish debate over the significance of the Jesus event. Increasingly, many Jewish sectors were no longer tolerant of the Way. They found themselves marginalized. Probably more disturbing to them than the loss of property was the loss of privilege and social acceptance among their fellow Israelites.

We can deduce from the Gospels that the majority of Jews among the populous held Jesus in high esteem. They may have been confused as to precisely who he was and what he was about, but for the most part they thought he was a good, godly, and important figure. Those who continued to take Jesus seriously had no problem receiving him as a prophet or holy man. They thought he was making a critical contribution to the political crisis that all of Palestine was embroiled in. Many among the Jews were cautiously following Jesus. They could fully embrace the Temple and the priesthood, the teaching of the Torah, and Jesus as a prophet or even the Messiah.

The crucifixion of Jesus and his subsequent resurrection changed all that. Jesus had a way of pushing the boundaries of what God was doing among his people beyond comfortable constructions. As the post-passion years increased so did the implications. It needs to be realized that the debate in the book of Hebrews is not between Jewish and Christian groups but between Jewish Christian groups. There was a different Jewish debate going on between the increasingly influential Pharisees and the Apostles. Although many Pharisees had an interest in Jesus they insisted that Jesus was only one of many contributing leaders but in no way a critical or central one. The Apostles were more and more realizing that Jesus was both the critical and central figure for the future of Israel. In the politically tumultuous years leading up to the Temple's destruction and the fall of Jerusalem the debate over Jesus became heated and bitter. More than likely, the group addressed in Hebrews found themselves in the middle. They still believed that Jesus was important, but they weren't sure they wanted to take Him as far as other Jewish believers were taking it. The Jewish opposition was saying, "Jesus is less than he claimed to be." The community of disciples was discovering that Jesus was even more than what they thought he was. The church in Hebrews was in between. They held that he was a significant contemporary figure alongside the temple, Torah, and priesthood. They found themselves increasingly marginalized by both the Pharisaic Jews and the Christian Jews. Both of these groups allowed for less and less 'middle ground'. The ramifications and implications wouldn't allow for it.

The people of this church found themselves in a crisis of indecision, and as with most major decisions, it much was at stake. The emerging rabbinic Judaism was increasingly hostile towards the Messianic Judaism of John the Baptist and Jesus. This was so much the case, especially with the embrace of Gentile believers, that the opposition began an agenda of labeling the movement "non-Jewish" or even worse, "anti-Jewish" As unfair and unreasonable as this propaganda was, it proved to be very effective. For one, it banded together the most antagonistic Jewish groups against the Christian Jews.

There were a couple of critical consequences the church of the Hebrews were intensely experiencing. The first one was psychological. These Jewish believers took their religion, faith, and history very seriously. They were struggling hard for the whole Jewish people for solutions that could carry them beyond this point of crisis. In a very odd twist by their opposition, they were now being left out of the arena all together. It must have been a severe emotional blow to be labeled an enemy to the state, a traitor, or an imposter. The second major consequence had even bigger ramifications for it brought Rome into the situation. By labeling the Messianic Jewish movement as non-Jewish, the early Christians found themselves outside the perimeters of officially sanctioned religions. This may not sound like much, but it meant the difference between freedom to openly practice religion and being an outlaw religion that not only had to be secretly practiced but could be aggressively shut down by civil authorities. Furthermore, it gave anybody opposing the Jesus movement a trump card that could bring down severe consequences.

Truly, these early believers could be put in the category of people mentioned above who were facing a restless, anxious, and stressful time. They too could have wondered if their God's Sabbath rest had eluded them. It may seem odd and even cruel the way the author of Hebrews approaches their situation, for he places the problem and solution squarely on their shoulders. Yes, he says, God has thrust you into the wilderness just like your fore fathers leaving Egypt. *Being in the wilderness* is a tough and unsettling experience, yet it is survivable; however, *wandering in the wilderness* is intolerable. It is critical to understand a bigger picture, to understand what is going on, and most importantly *where one is going.* This is where the Hebrew church is failing; they have lost their target and goal. They aren't keeping their eyes on their destination, and because of that, God's real and abiding rest is eluding them *regardless of their outward situation.*

Two Way Wilderness - Choose your Phobia

Therefore, while the promise of entering his rest remains, let us fear lest any of you be judged to have failed to reach it.[50]

In the cartoon *A Charlie Brown's Christmas,* Charlie Brown is depressed about Christmas. He knows this isn't right, so for five cents, he seeks the counsel of Lucy at her psychologist stand. At one point she rattles off a list of "phobias" and asks Charlie to pick the one that fits him best. Lucy's

---

[50] Hebrew 4:1

God's Restless Rest

solution for Charlie it seems was to accurately pinpoint what he was afraid of.

Chapter 4 begins with an odd injunction, one that doesn't immediately seem compatible with rest. The imperative is to "be afraid." A phobia of any kind is usually an unsettling thing. Phobias make us guarded, defensive, protective, and withdrawn. None of this is compatible with Sabbath rest. Ironically, the writer exhorts his listeners to be anxious about anxiety, restless about rest or weary of weariness. In a real sense, the writer of Hebrews exhorts his readers to have "katapausiphobia" – the fear of not finding rest. Actually, however, it is a fear of being lost, of wandering without direction. It does seem odd, but the gist is this: If one's life is without the rest – Sabbath rest – found in God, if one is not experiencing it, living it, and moving towards it, if one's life is not squarely focused on the One from whom all blessings flow, then that is something truly to worry about. That is a wandering, empty, barren, and desolate place to be, as the author of Hebrews reminds his audience of the 40 years in the wilderness. It means one has seized up in the wandering desolation of indecision.

> *Who were they who heard and rebelled? Were they not all those Moses led out of Egypt? And with whom was he angry for forty years? Was it not with those who sinned, whose bodies fell in the desert?*[51]

The author's comparison of the church situation and the Israelites in the wilderness under Moses is more than casual metaphor and deeper than simile. In the time of Jesus and the apostolic church, most of the Jewish world had an anxious preoccupation concerning the future of Israel. Although there were a wide variety of opinions as to what was or should happen, most parties in the debate felt something was going to happen, something had to give. As N.T. Wright has aptly pointed out, many Jews of the time felt that they had never really returned from the exile, even though they were in the land.[52] This position was deeply felt mainly because even though they were in the land, they did not rule in it.

At this time, there was a revival of interest in the ancient Israelite traditions. There were many 'back to' movements: back to Abraham, back to Enoch, back to the patriarchs, back to Moses etc. All of these movements were seeking to bring into the contemporary scene something genuine, pure, innocent and lost into what many perceived as a confused and corrupt situation. Jesus began his public ministry under the auspices of one such "back to" movement. It was lead by John the Baptist and it could be called the "back to the exodus" or more accurately "back to the wilderness"

---

[51] Hebrews 3:16-17
[52] N.T. Wright, The *New Testament and the People of God*, pg243; Fortress Press

movement. It was a confident belief that God's time to move his people out of their bondage was now and that God would do it as he did before in Egypt and Babylon; he would lead them out first into the wilderness and then into the promised land. The first Christians seized and owned the metaphor of a new exodus and wilderness experience. "In the wilderness, prepare the way of the Lord," was their rallying call, "and there you will meet God on the march." It is no slight coincidence that the writers of Hebrews and the gospel bring up the wilderness tradition.

The wilderness tradition found in the Old Testament is a bit bi-polar. Depending on how one looked at it, it was the best of times and the worst of times. Although there was a terrible failure on the part of the generation that left Egypt, including Moses, one can find fond nostalgia around it too. Quite a bit of romanticism around those wilderness years is found, and surprisingly, it is mostly God who expresses fond memories of it. These recollections are spoken of only in powerful and intimate relational terms. God sentimentally speaks of that time as a loving father recalls the proper raising of a firstborn son.[53] Like a shepherd leading his flock was that time when the Lord *guided them safely* through the fright of the desolate unknown.[54] Finding Israel in the wilderness *was like finding grapes in the desert and seeing the early fruit on the fig tree.*[55]

It is in the disgust of Israel's blatant sins and the horrors of exile that the prophets dream of going back to the wilderness. For all its failures, the wilderness experience was a time of raw and essential relational encounter and dependency, stripped of all distraction and preoccupation. Going through the desert means hardcore dependency.

This wilderness experience is also spoken of as the most wonderful time in a person's life: courtship, that place of young, stary-eyed, innocent and heart throbbing love.[56] The great thing about 'falling in love' is that it is almost entirely devoid of life's complications. Certainly, finding a partner will lead to enduring together all the pitfalls of this earthly life, yet for a brief season, one looks upon his partner not in terms of who they really are, but in terms of what their love wants them to be. In this sense, love truly is blind. The picture of the wilderness is one in which God looks upon Israel not in terms of what it was or what He knows she will become, but only in terms of what He wants her to be: pure, innocent, beautiful. In the wilderness, God fell in love with Israel and thus made Israel a virgin, even though she wasn't. For

---

[53] Deuteronomy 8:1-5, 29:5
[54] Psalm 78:52
[55] Hosea 9:10
[56] Hosea 2:14-23

the prophets, the wilderness represents raw and intimate relationship with the Lord and the place of second chances, new beginnings, and fresh starts.[57]

Both the first and the second wilderness generations probably didn't enjoy that experience. It was a time of severe testing and a most unsettling experience. The author of Hebrews, however, sees a night and day difference in the way the faithful respond in such situations. If we take our clue from chapter 4 verse 1, on the one hand there were those who had a casual view towards the rest God was providing. On the other hand, there were those whose fear of not having rest and of remaining in an unsettled place caused them to avail themselves of every opportunity to have it, both in the wilderness and into the promise land. Both generations earnestly desired rest, but the first generation could only look behind or around them to envision it. Unbelievably, they thought the best opportunity for rest was in the land of perpetual work! Equally wrongheaded was the attempt to *settle down in the wilderness.* Because the second generation accepted the rest provided in the wilderness, they were motivated to move towards a more permanent, secure, and abiding rest.

The irony of the wilderness experience is that God led them into a very uneasy situation, and from all appearances it was not very restful. It would have been a ready temptation for any of us to question the sufficiency of this god to follow through with what got started. In that situation, God provided rest for them, but even there, many people wouldn't take God up on it. The writer of Hebrews reiterates the theme already covered under Sabbath rest. Just as Shabbat is established in the midst of chaos, in the middle of the Ten Words, in the heat of contraversy with the Pharisees, so it is found in the middle of the wilderness, surrounded by barrenness, hostility and depravity.

The Israelites in the wilderness, as well as the Church addressed in Hebrews, were being asked to enter both the rest currently offered by God in the wilderness and to keep moving towards a rest that awaits them. Indeed their mini-rest in the wilderness should have served as a prime motivator to keep moving. Paradoxically, it was a rest on the run. It is an unsettled settlement. They failed to see that their God was on the move, that Papa was a rolling stone. Like the guiding pillar of the exodus and the spinning wheels of the exile[58], the Lord would not settle for unsettlement. He is restless about his rest.

God is not finished with human history yet. All of human history is moving towards its rest in God, but until all is completed, God is not done with his work. Ironically, Shabbat, established on the seventh day of creation, serves as the evidence that God is still working in human history and this business

---

[57] Isaiah 35
[58] Ezekiel 1

is unfinished. The author urges his listeners to rest in the assurance that God's work in the world is on schedule and is moving towards its Shabbat just as it was in creation.[59]

Sabbath Rest – The Eternal Day Has Begun

Today, if you hear his voice,
do not harden your hearts
as you did in the rebellion
during the time of testing in the desert[60]

The church in the book of Hebrews was facing a crisis of time, not in terms of time management but in terms of a crisis of history. There are probably no other people on the planet who have defined themselves so profoundly by their sense of historical remembrance as the Jews. As with many Jews today, so it was with the Jewish Christians in the early church. The very understanding of who they are is deeply engrained in whom they have been. There was a first century Jew from Galilee that seemed to know that history in an extraordinary and passionate way. He seemed to know it as if he had lived all of it. He talked as if he knew and had been there with Abraham, Moses and David. He seemed intimately familiar with the struggle and suffering of Moses, Elijah, Isaiah, and Jeremiah, but most of all, he was familiar with God's strife in redeeming his people.

The predicament of these Christians was a crisis of time. There was a growing anxiety in which their experience of Jesus had brought them into a sense of discontinuity with their past. I'm reminded of a similar experience of the American Indian in which much of their crisis was brought on not just with the loss of land and place, but with what those things meant as far as continuity of being and identity. They were losing their sense of place in time, in history.[61] Their "maps of the past" were being decimated. Perhaps, more than any other transience that they were feeling, the early Jewish Christians were feeling restlessness brought on by their encounter with Jesus that had thrust them into confusion over their place in time

It was a stroke of strategic genius that the author of Hebrews addresses the crisis in the church by referencing Psalm 95, for he spans the spectrum of time from the creation of the world to today. He seeks to establish in the

---

[59] Hebrews 4:4-6
[60] Psalms 95 and Hebrews 3:8
[61] "We have maps of the past. We have history, but not as most people understand history. We have places…these things that we can identify with in terms of time and experience." *M. Scott Momaday in* Ken Burns, *The West: Episode 2, Empire Upon the Trails,* PBS Home Video

God's Restless Rest

hearts of his readers that the rest established by God on the seventh day is available now and also serves as a sign or referent to a more permanent, glorious, and abiding rest. There is coming a day when God will rest from his work in human history. Indeed, that day has begun in Jesus. It will be a day that will read similarly to the creation story. "On the Day God finished doing everything he planned for the history of mankind, when all things had come to pass and everything was put in order, God stopped working and rested." The Sabbath day should serve as a signpost of where the people of God are going, not where they've been.

It is amazing how unreligious the Sabbath command is in the Torah, yet it is readily apparent that the Sabbath day formed the incentive for the people of God to gather together for worship. All such gatherings and especially the seasonal pilgrimages to the holy places were critical times to renew the covenant relationship with their God. Covenant renewal was a critical act of worship. It was a time to recall the mighty deeds of God that brought them into a relationship with him; far more important than recalling those events however, the covenant renewal was the vehicle to pull the contemporary generation *into that experience.* The covenant renewal was a time for all the participants to re-member themselves to the great acts of God towards their people. It was a time for them to walk where their ancestors had walked. They too were to brush blood on the doorposts, to quickly pack only necessities, worship God in the wilderness, stand before the fire-filled mountain and tremble, and to decide whether to believe the spies reports of the Promised Land.

Psalm 95 was composed to invite and bind the Israelites who are settled in the Promised Land to their history. It not only takes the contemporary audience to the past, it brings the past into the present and future of Israel. The first part of the Psalms is a great convocation to worship their God. *Come let us sing for joy to the Lord...Come let us worship and bow down!* It is no wonder that this Psalm became a favorite prayer used to inaugurate the Shabbat. The tradition is ancient and is still apart of both Jewish and Christian traditions today. This psalm would deeply resonate for the little Jewish church in Hebrews for it could be heard in the Temple during the temple service for the Sabbath day.[62] It was both an invitation to worship and to usher in Shabbat.

The invitation to worship the Lord and remember the covenant in the Psalm also incites crisis: *Today...do not harden your hearts.* It brings the contemporary listeners into the crisis of decision their ancestors faced in the wilderness. Now, they too must decide what they must do. It takes them back to the crisis of indecision faced in the wilderness and makes it a

---

[62] F.F. Bruce, Hebrews, *The New International Commentary of the New Testament* pg63

contemporary crisis. They too must decide; will we go on as God's people, accept our plight as necessary, and keep looking ahead to where God is taking us?

An author once labeled the Old Testament a 'text in travail'. This, I find, to be a most appropriate designation for from Genesis to Malachi, God's spirit is 'stirring' over chaos. There is an underlying and persistent struggle that never seems to cease. Even when the Israelites get to the land and establish themselves to a height of glory and security there is an uneasy and precarious sense that God has not gotten his people where he wants them to be. It is as ironic and almost humorous how the book of Judges recycles the same theme, "When the Israelites got secure and comfortable, they went back to their old ways and then everything falls apart and God starts over again." At the pinnacle of the Israelites' glory, as Solomon prays before the glory shrouded temple, he can only appeal for God's mercy because he can already sense in himself and his people that their propensity is to degenerate. All through the ancient history of Israel there is an agonizing sense that Israel could never quite get to their manifest destiny. Perhaps, in a trivial way, Cub or Red Sox fans know that feeling. There is a sense of unfulfillment even in the land under the monarchy.

In the middle of the warm and exciting call to worship found in Psalm 95, there is an abrupt shift that almost seems rude. It is as if to say, God is great and worthy of full attention, so get you act together NOW!" In the midst of the liturgical community, the Psalm draws the worshippers into God's time, into eternal history. The Psalm binds creative and human history to God's schedule and his timetable. It compels the worshipping community to engage God's history from creation, to the Israelites in the wilderness, in the land, in exile, in the new exodus - the gospel of Jesus -, the rise of the Church and its orthodoxy and even into the twenty-first century. God's work in human history, however, will not be complete until "all things are put under his feet".

It is in the author's (both of the Psalm and Hebrews) emphasis on "today" where the language of rest is revisited. Shabbat - ceasing time - is the day of days to stop what you're doing and be orientated toward the One who really matters. The biblical notion of rest is basic and consistent throughout. Be reminded, first of all, that rest is most often referred as 'my rest', i.e. God's rest. Rest is a settled place. It is to be settled down, free from the fear of attack from enemies or the vulnerability and exposure from the wilderness. It is most profoundly a sense of finding one's home. It is home, a place of blessing and belonging. Important for the current discussion, rest in the biblical sense is not only something worth having and enjoying, but it is also used in the sense of something *worth journeying towards*, i.e. Jerusalem. There is no better referent to biblical rest than in Naomi's wish for Ruth:

God's Restless Rest

May the Lord grant that each of you will find rest in the home of another husband.[63]

To return to the first illustration of the chapter, apparently it really was the case that some of the wagon trains moving across the western territories had vicious debates about whether to stop traveling on Shabbat.[64] This appropriately gives us a picture of rest to be had now as well as rest as a destination to be moving towards. God would have us choose to take sabbatical stops along the way to our truest and finest resting place. Those stops along the way in fact become critical, for they help constitute the kind of disposition that generates and moves toward the best rest.

By referencing Psalm 95 the writer reminds the early Jewish Christians as well as any other believers of any generation of a great failure. The wilderness was not a mistake on God's part. There was no other way for the Israelites to get to the Promised Land. The mistake of the wilderness was a failure to trust God, and especially to trust God to follow through. It was a failure to see beyond the giants in front of them. To "believe" in God meant that *testing* and *resting* can happen simultaneously.

Rest for the author of Hebrews has to do with vision. It is not only an ability to see beyond the immediate situation, but it is also to see that the history of God's people and what God is doing in the world extends beyond human history. It is something that is happening with God since the 7th day of creation. God's rest, the writer emphasizes, is something God currently enjoys and is open, made available to all. Ironically, it is something also to strive for, to earnestly pursue. It is a primary component of human history as well as eternal history. Most critical for the struggling Christian, however, is to perceive that God's rest has been established since the seventh day of creation and is now open to them.[65] This is the whole stress on "today" and "now," for God's Sabbath rest is prime time or the opportune time. Sabbath day is not only in the middle of creation history and human history, it is also in the middle of human history and eternal history. It is where the two converge. When we stop to rest, it is also where our present time converges with the eternal present.

"Today" – Shabbat – is the day of days, the opportune time, to enter into a rest that God has, is and will forever enjoy. But it can only be seen and experienced in trust, neither by angry demand nor by fatalistic resignation. God's rest is open now, but only to those who trust Him and his sufficiency and ability to follow through with the complete plan of salvation. Ironically, God's rest requires something from us; we must strive for it. It requires

---

[63] Ruth 1:9
[64] Ken Burns, *The West,* episode 3, PBS Home Video
[65] Hebrews 4:1

trusting response. I have often wondered if Michael Angelo understood something of this seeming contradiction in his famous painting *The Creation of Adam*. There it is pictured a striving reach of both God and man towards each other, yet God is reclined.

There is one thing that prevents us from experiencing God's rest according to the author of Hebrews; it is unbelief. We must be careful, however, that we stick to the author's understanding of disobedience and unbelief. In the passage, unbelief is understood as not responding to the relief God was offering. They couldn't see that God was reaching out to them from his Sabbath rest and to it. The kind of unbelief is not so much a wanting to go back to things as much as not wanting to go forward. It is short-circuiting a process that is already put in motion.

Their unbelief is also called disobedience. Disobedience is associated with not fully embracing the message they had received. Obedience is trusting in the word brought to them by a reliable and proven source. The wavering on the part of the Hebrew church revolved around a question about Jesus. Just how far was Jesus to be trusted above and beyond the time tested and proven authority of Moses. They too were questioning, as were the Israelites in the wilderness, "Is the Lord God with us or not?"

The truth of this is as valid today as it was nearly two thousand years ago. God's rest is available today, right NOW! Nearly everyone waivers in a struggle. It is natural to relate those struggles to a desert experience: alone, destitute, desperate, and not sure what to do or who to be mad at. We are as susceptible to a loss of confidence in God's ability as those ancient Israelites who walked by the bodies of the Egyptian firstborn and through walls of water. The message is the same: what matters more than faltering yesterday is trusting Him today! Now is as good as time as any, precisely because God's rest has been established since the seventh day and marched on through the dark day of crucifixion into the glorious new day of resurrection morning.

Jesus –The Rising of the New Sabbath Day.

The church in the book of Hebrews must be decisive. They must get themselves out of "option lock." Most importantly, however, they need not deliberate over who they are, what their circumstance is, or who is opposing them. As critical as these things may be, the author doesn't bother with them. He squarely and consistently places the crisis of decision on one thing. *They must decide on who they understand Jesus to be.* They wanted to stop when God wasn't stopping. Ironically then, God's rest can elude us when we are trying to stop when God isn't. God's work in Jesus didn't stop with his birth, his first visit to the temple, or his itinerate preaching ministry

God's Restless Rest

in Galilee. It didn't stop amidst the rising contention with competing Jewish parties. It didn't stop with the high-pitched crisis of the Passion Week, the crucifixion or burial. No, Jesus rose from the dead and ascended into heaven. He is alive, clothed in honor, and sitting (reposed?) in the eternal presence of his Father. Jesus had pushed the boundaries of conventional Judaism. This did not make it non-Judaism, anti-Judaism, reformed Judaism or even revolutionary Judaism; it made it fulfilled, transcendent, and eternal Judaism. Out of this one man's story, Jesus, the story of mankind and of God's people past, present, and future is blessed. This is precisely where the church was faltering. They were baulking at the *full implications of the Christ events* in the same way that their Israelite ancestors had refused to embrace the full implications of the Passover and the Reed Sea.

Their restlessness, the author insists, is self-inflicted. Having come this far with Jesus, they find themselves resistant to go on with Him. For them, Jesus was a promising figure, a holy man, a prophet, a charismatic and compassionate political leader, and a wise man, but was he an extra-ordinary man, a divine and now eternal man? Also, if he is now eternally glorified, then what was he *before* his earthly life? The author persists in framing up their dilemma solely in these terms: "fix your eyes on Jesus". Look *fully on Him*. The question for these believers was whether or not God really had thrown all of his marbles into this one basket, and brought all of salvation history to a climax in and through His son Jesus Christ?

These early Christians seized up when it came to developing the full picture of who Jesus must truly be. They didn't want to follow through with the full implications of their decision in Jesus. It is not enough to just decide to follow Jesus; *one must also define the Jesus one is going to follow*. This is true today as it was for the early Jewish believers. The more one is willing to embrace the full implications of who Jesus is, was, and is to come, the more one is able to keep moving towards one's resting place. We too can seize up when we fix our eyes on only one aspect of the true and fullest reality of Jesus. Our spiritual growth is equal to our view of Jesus relative to time: what he was - pre-existent Word; what he is - earthly man and ascended man; and what he is to come - all things under his rule and him acknowledged as ruler of all.

Having a full picture of Jesus may seem like lofty and heady theological deliberation that does not relate to the common Christian's daily struggle and life, but this is precisely where the author of Hebrew's places it. A clear and complete understanding of Jesus was also the struggle of the early church for the first four centuries and it had huge implications. As to finding rest in a fast-paced and restless world and a world that increasingly suffers from historical amnesia, our picture of the time-fulfilling Christ and the "historical Jesus" is critical. It behooves us to take note of what the author accentuates about Jesus. In this regard, he focuses intensely on the high priestly status of Jesus. To this we will now look.

Jesus the Christ – "The Perfect Situation"

My wife and I have had a long and fond friendship with another couple. Once, we had spontaneously invited them to go out for the evening with us. Brian was grateful for the invitation, but they declined saying that they were already "settled in for the evening." We have always chuckled about that, for we can easily picture Brian and Carla in their cozy living room, snuggled up in their ergonomically worn chairs with blanket, books, and tea all necessarily near. They were perfectly situated and had no need to undo that.

As a young Christian, our youth group would sing a song from Psalm 25. As was sometimes the case, we sang parts that I didn't understand. The song was about Jerusalem. It went:

> *Great is the Lord and greatly to be praised,*
> *In the city of our God, in the mountain of his holiness,*
> *Beautiful for situation, the joy of the whole earth,*
> *Is Mount Zion on the sides of the north the city of the great King?*

The term *beautiful for situation* had somewhat stumped me. What does that mean? I've come to understand that it is talking about a perfect situation or setup. It means something similar to what is mentioned on the seventh day of creation in Genesis. Since God had created all things in a strategic and organized way and had ingeniously placed every assembly piece in its perfect place, God could stop, sit back in his lawn chair and satisfyingly say, "Aah, it is finished. It's perfect." God and his world are "settled in" and therefore perfectly situated for a peaceful and long-lasting relationship. In a similar way, the Psalmist speaks of God being perfectly situated among his people. When the set up of God ruling from His temple in Zion is right, it is *the joy of the whole earth.*

There is no other place in the New Testament where such an emphasis is placed on the role of Jesus as a priest, let alone the high priest. Yet the writer of Hebrews concentrates exclusively on this role. It is in believing that Jesus is the high priest for his people that the early church finds its sedative for their unnerving situation. Even in their anxiety, he exhorts them, they must come to understand that the eternal rest in God is already open because Jesus is now "perfectly situated" to bring God's history with His people and humankind to its completion, to its final Day, its Sabbath rest. Although we aren't there yet, we can *rest assured* that Jesus is.

As with other aspects of Israel's history, the history of the priesthood was dubious and marked by corruption and failure. Its official beginnings with

Aaron and the Levites did not fair well. It didn't take Aaron long to succumb to the idolistic leanings of a stubborn congregation. The Levites carried on that marred tradition in the period of the judges, and by the time it gets to Samuel, Eli and his sons are hopelessly corrupt. The questionable history continues on into the period of monarchical strength, with the priestly class easily changing from Baal to Yahweh and back again whenever it was most expedient. It is in fact because of the ever-present tendency toward waywardness that the rise of prophets occurs.

The priesthood was not completely devoid of quality leadership. Among the more shining examples are Samuel and Ahimelech in the time of the early monarchy. The priests were in fact behind many of the reformation movements during the monarchical period. Ezekiel was a key figure during the exile as a priestly prophet, and Ezra was the leading figure in guiding the people in the land post-exile.

The importance of the priesthood and the leadership of the high priest do not take prominence until the complete and devastating collapse of the monarchy during the exile. From Samuel up to that point, the locus of leadership for God's people was definitively on God's messiah, the king. The other major venues of spiritual guidance, prophets, priests, and wise men, only held significance in relationship to the king and his agenda. Because of the leadership void left after the exile, it became incumbent upon the priests to take a more prominent leadership function. The priestly class becomes the predominant and authoritative leadership in the post-exilic period all the way up to the time of Jesus.

The idea of a priestly leader or priestly king was not foreign to Israel. All the great leaders of Israel: Abraham, Israel, Moses, Samuel, David, Solomon, Josiah and others performed critical priestly functions. Key among these was the role of intercessor. At the time of Jesus and the apostolic church, the high priest was the most prominent figure of authority and leadership for the Jewish people. Although the whole priestly structure was viewed quite negatively by many Jews for its corruption and compromise with Rome, even the most vehement of opposition was not looking for the demise of the high priest as much as a radical reform and replacement of it.

For many devout Jewish Christians of this time it would have been simply inconceivable to think of any important Jewish leader as abrogating the authority of the high priest. Not even Jesus, Peter, or Paul dared show disrespect to that position. The fall of Jerusalem in A.D. 70 drastically reshuffled the cards. The Roman soldiers virtually dismantled the whole priestly apparatus along with the destruction of the temple and Jerusalem. Once again, God's people found themselves in a leadership vacuum. They were splintered into vicious and competing agendas. Leadership and authority had no clear and decisive expression and the history of God's people seemed once again fractured and without direction.

Oddly enough, the early Christians saw in these events a great work of God in progress. Yes, the beheading of John the Baptist, the crucifixion of Jesus, and the death of Stephen and James were terrible, yet there was something extraordinary happening that didn't just keep them going, it jettisoned them forward with an invigorated sense of destiny. They saw God on the move. Even more so, they *profoundly understood what God was doing in all of this*. This was *the message* that was told to the Hebrew's church, and they were having second thoughts about it. Just as God masterfully designed and assembled the elements of creation, the author is urging the church to be confident that He is doing the same with Israel's history in Jesus Christ. In Jesus, God is assembling all the seemingly despairing and disassembled elements of the human story into a unity, a harmony, and a cohesive whole. All things would come together in Him, and because of His ascended and glorified status Jesus was in the perfect situation to make all of it happen. God, in Jesus the Christ, is taking all the broken and tormented pieces of Israel's story and gluing them back together into a glorious and harmonious relationship with God. As God's high priest, Jesus is the One to unify Israel's tormented past, her present crisis, and her destiny. He is the One to rule and administrate over "the perfect situation."

The author accentuates several aspects of Jesus' high priestly role to persuade them to fully embrace (believe) the message they have heard. It is critical to understand where Jesus is *now* and what he is doing *presently*. It would do us well to take to heart this appeal, because much of twentieth century scholarship has fallen into the same debacle as these early Christians. They have disassociated the earthly man, Jesus the Galilean, with the heavenly and glorified man, Christ. The early Christians made no mistake when they repeatedly combined the name Jesus with Christ. They were and are inseparable. The author needs to equally persuade the contemporary audience as he did the first century one that the ascended and glorified Christ *is the historical Jesus*. They were tempted to shortcut the historical process, being willing to accept Him as temporal messiah but not the transcendent one. This impasse, the author insists, is what makes for a most anxious and restless situation, like wandering in the wilderness. It simply won't do, and it is simply not true. He exhorts his listeners to *fix their eyes upon Jesus*, both then and now, in order to fully see how God is bringing things together in Him.

First, Jesus is perfectly situated because he brings a unity to the disparity between priestly class and "laity." In his suffering, he became *like his brethren*. In this, he addressed two major problems of the High Priest of the first century: internal corruption and a disassociation (lack of empathy) with the Jewish people at large.

Strong was the opposition's point that Jesus' suffering and death was a clear sign of God's disapproval, and it therefore disqualified him as a true leader of God's people. This probably would be true if Jesus had not been raised from the dead, but since he has, the truth is just the opposite. God has vindicated his messiah, defeated his fiercest enemy, and placed him on a seat of glory and honor.

Jesus therefore, has addressed one of the most precarious predicaments of any kind of leadership. It is one that is raising its ugly head in much of our contemporary life. How does one oversee a situation, which means to stand above it, while at the same time being sensitive and aware of the people one is leading? Somehow we want strong, brilliant and decisive leadership that doesn't lose site of the common man's situation. Jesus didn't earn his credentials as high priest because of lineage, wealth, status, or education. He is not a professional or expert high priest. No, his elevation to the office of intercessor for his people came through his patient endurance and long-suffering. It came as it did his ancient predecessor found in the book of Isaiah, not by great military conquest but by a willingness to suffer with the shame of his people and the shameful rejection by his people.[66]

In this regard, Jesus' humble life and suffering was not a sign of weakness but one of strength. He knows our human struggle and pain to the core. He did not live isolated or insulated from the pain of human existence. *Since the children have flesh and blood, he too shared in their humanity...For this reason he had to be made like his brothers in every way, in order that he might become a merciful and faithful high priest.*[67] Unobtrusively, we visit again the language of rest. Jesus is the true image-bearer, the clearest expression of what Adam was meant to be. He is the fullest expression of humanity and can be the guiding, empathetic and trustworthy light to lead out of any human dilemma. He didn't fail like Moses did in the wilderness or like any human leader for that matter. He led his people while never separating himself from them. The New Testament is adamant about this point: he could have saved himself, but he did not. If he had, he could still be high priest, but he would have been like every other human leader: great but out of touch with those whom he is leading, serving, and administrating over.

Second, Jesus is perfectly situated to unify Israel's fractured history. He makes sense out of what has happened in the past, what happened with his earthly ministry, and what will be Israel's ultimate destiny.

The high priest and temple rubric employed in Hebrews is designed to show decisively Jesus' continuity, and more importantly, his unity with time.

---

[66] Isaiah 53
[67] Hebrews 2:14, 17

These early Jewish believers knew that historically speaking the authority of Moses ultimately resided with the high priest. This could not be sidestepped by anyone. They had come to believe that God was doing something important in Jesus, but they were uncertain as to how far that went. The author of Hebrews wants to show that Jesus has authority as high priest not because he broke with the past, but because he was and is consistent with it. "Now of Christ – past, present, and future *are* tied together in a glorious unity."[68] There is a unity between the Jesus of time and the timeless Christ. In this case, out of the one who is ever present – hence the "today" emphasis – the many (through all of human history) are blessed. This powerfully relates to the understanding of Shabbat going back to Genesis one. Essentially, Shabbat is God's gracious turning to mankind's story, their history. To extend this from the Hebrews passage, Shabbat is God's gracious turning to **all of human history, just as it is God's affirmation towards all of creation.**

Perhaps this seems like pie-in-the-sky theology that doesn't relate much to contemporary struggles, but this is precisely what the church in Hebrews was missing. The intervention of the man Jesus in first century Palestine enabled him to bring every situation into continuity with eternal history, into the eternal story. Jesus, as a permanent ruling priest, is perfectly situated to make sense of and give meaning to the human story. This is mainly so because he clearly points to Israel and humankind's ultimate destiny.

As this relates to the wilderness experience brought up in Hebrews chapter three, the Israelites failed to trust their God that he was leading them not only to a physical place of rest, but also to a place of rest in history and in the grand scheme of things.

Third, because of his suffering and death, Jesus is perfectly situated to unify the disparity between the necessity for purity when administering justice and holiness and the overpowering propensity toward corruption. Although animal sacrifices could aid in bringing sobriety to those approaching a sovereign, they still proved ineffective. Corruption diminishes the effectual power of sacrifice. Sacrifice is inextricably connected to the role of intercession. Someone who stands in the middle of warring parties must have some acceptability to both sides. Otherwise, he will only compound the problem. Jesus didn't just offer his life for others; there have been plenty of people who have done the same. It was the kind of life offered that makes all the difference. It was *an indestructible life,*[69] *willingly offered through the eternal Spirit*, and by faithful obedience was *unblemished to God.*[70]

---

[68] James D.G. Dunn, *Unity and Diversity in the New Testament, pg* 288; Trinity Press Int.
[69] Hebrews 7:16
[70] Hebrews 9:14

Finally, Jesus brings together the divided and contentious history of leadership in Israel. He fulfills the role of interceding on behalf of his people. He unifies the disparity between sitting on the mercy seat and dispensing mercilessness. There was a time in Israel under David and Solomon where there was a unity to Israel's leadership. God's anointed one was a mighty savior and deliverer like Moses and Joshua. He administered justice, law, and order like Moses and Samuel. Like Aaron and Samuel, he organized and performed important sacrifices and covenant-renewal festivals. He presided over the temple and its operations. He also instituted the school and office of wisdom. Like Abraham, Joseph, Moses, Samuel, David, Elijah and the prophets, the messiah was a charismatic leader directed by God's Spirit and guided by visions and zeal for what God wanted to accomplish.

Mainly because of sin and arrogance, leadership in Israel split up into various components. The unique role of *messiah* no longer operated as a unifying leader. The king still was the main leader for military and administrative office, but the prophetic function of the messiah, beginning with Nathan, was separate from kingship and became its antagonistic watchdog and corrective. Although the priestly class had to work more closely with the king than prophets, they were often unable to maintain the proper sense of the Lord's holiness and glory. The wisdom school often provided counsel devoid of its central component, which was "the fear of the Lord." The varying roles of the Messiah developed separate histories and traditions through the exile and the return into the land.

Although our American idea of leadership is to divide power into various counter-balances, the ancient Israelites did not view this as the *perfect situation*. Yes, counterbalances can be a corrective, but they can also work against each other until the nation is frozen and powerless to act wisely and decisively. Perhaps idealistically, many Israelites were looking for a messiah who would unite the divided and contentious functions of national leadership into a harmonious whole guided predominantly by God's Spirit.

This is precisely why the author of Hebrews brings in the ancient figure of Melchizedek. As mentioned earlier, at the time of Jesus there where many "back to" movements. They sought to bring into the contemporary crisis something original or authentic about Israel's faith that was considered lost. Most of these movements focused on some key figure who most accentuated some lost aspect. Curiously, these figures were mainly pre-Moses leaders. Also, their mention in the Bible is somewhat cryptic and mysterious. Enoch, for instance, held a huge preoccupation with many. Melchizedek fits into this need for authentic figureheads quite nicely. Most importantly, Melchizedek provides a picture for understanding just how Jesus is perfectly set up to bring peace to all the chaotic elements of our human experience.

Melchizedek represents a return to a purer form or more exalted ideal of a ruler, for he was a priestly king. Psalm 110, which is quoted by the author of Hebrews as well as Jesus, provides clear evidence that the notion of *messiah* combined the roles of a mighty warrior and powerful ruler with that of an interceding priest. Melchizedek ruled over the *city of peace* with strength, wisdom, and glory. Psalm 110 demonstrates that the Israelites always had a notion of a priestly ruler. By solemn oath the Lord proclaims that the king of Israel is *a priest forever in the order of Melchizedek.* It appears that as far back as can be remembered, the Israelites greatly admired the kind of king Melchizedek seemed to be. Certainly, Melchizedek was viewed idealistically; nonetheless, the vision is for a charismatic ruler who has subjugated all things, defeated enemies, set up a place and situation to hear intercession, and then hears the needs of the people. Like Melchizedek, this unique person would lead with vision, drive, and inspiration.

Once again, we are revisited by the notion that *out of the one the many are blessed.* Ultimately, and most importantly, a priestly ruler like Melchizedek sits on the *throne of grace.* To sit on the throne may sound glorious and luxurious, but it was a precarious place to be for it meant *standing in the middle, filling the gap between forces that are at odds with each other.* Once again we visit a central idea around Sabbath rest: it is that thing in the middle of seemingly incongruent and conflicting forces. It is the ballast that brings equilibrium to what would be a chaotic and uncontrollable situation. The ultimate role of the king in Israel is plainly expressed in Solomon's prayer at the inauguration of the temple:

> Give attention to your servant's prayer and his plea for mercy, O Lord our God. Hear the cry and the prayer that your servant is praying in your presence this day...Hear the supplication of your servant and of your people Israel when they pray toward this place. Hear from heaven, your dwelling place, and when you hear, forgive.[71]

The messiah's most important function was to intercede, conciliate, and go between the precarious relationship between a holy God and a sin-prone people. His primary task was to humbly beseech God's help – seek mercy. The throne of grace is a place where one who is overwhelmed by a life threatening ordeal or situation can make an appeal for favorable outside intervention. Critical to an appeal to mercy is the belief on the part of the one seeking it that he/she is powerless to correct the situation on their own and that the one dispensing mercy is powerful enough to make something happen.

---

[71] 1 Kings 8:28-30

Like Melchizedek, Jesus brings together into one all the elements of the fractured leadership roles in Israel and concentrates his role most importantly on interceding between God and his people. Contrary to our contemporary notions of how things should be, Jesus in his role as high priest brings a unity between church and state, between our common everyday affairs and eternal ones. Even more so than his predecessors, Jesus no longer makes his appeals from the awkward position of the inadequacy of his own life and from the crude place of a temple built with stones. No, Jesus *has gone through the heavens*. He has already entered the promise land, his home, that perfect place of rest where one can perpetually draw nearer to the source of Life. Even though we aren't there yet, Jesus is now perfectly situated to bring all competing and contentious polarities into a harmony and a unity of purpose.

Conclusion

There are many, many troubles in this life. No one eludes them, and for the most part, troubles are self-induced whether individually or collectively. There are many ways that we are seeking rest in the midst of them. Unfortunately, many of our solutions are only compounding our restlessness and anxiety. Many alternatives for relief may in fact provide some temporary fix, but cannot possibly lead us toward a real and abiding rest when they are not squarely centered on the One who is the very meaning of the word. The recipients of the book of Hebrews, as well as us, must have eyes to see beyond our own situation, beyond our own sense of time and importance. Rest will elude anyone who doesn't understand – believe and obey- that Jesus Christ is at the very center of what is really real. Jesus Christ is neither some extra element in life nor is he on the periphery. Rest eluded the church in Hebrews because they weren't willing or able to see that *God made known to us the mystery of his will according to his good pleasure, which he purposed in Christ, to be put into effect when the times will have reached their fulfillment –* **to bring all things in heaven and on earth together under one head, even Christ**[72] God is moving everything going on in human history toward this rest. Happy, blessed and rested are those in the wilderness who keep their destination always before them.

Wandering pilgrim, find here a home.
Wandering pilgrim, find here a home.
Wandering pilgrim, find here a home.

---

[72] Ephesians 1:9-10

Lay down your sorrows, your worries and woes.[73]

Let us who mystically,
Represent the cherubim.
And sing the thrice-holy hymn,
to the life creating Trinity.
Now set aside all earthly cares,
Set aside all earthly cares.[74]

---

[73] Worship song; origin unknown
[74] Divine Liturgy of St. Chrysostum

CAN REST BE DONE?
THOUGHTS ON SHABBAT

So, how does someone "do" rest, God's rest? It has been a critique of my teaching that I'm not very practical. I don't really bring the Scriptural teaching down to application. I admit that I have a hard time with this. I blame some of it on the Bible itself, most of which is not immediately applicable. It seems to me that a large portion of the Bible is trying to get us to see something, more than to do something. Even so, I'm not always sure myself what all a Scriptural teaching like this one should mean. For sure, a Jew or Catholic would read this in quite a different way than a Protestant. As has already been the case, it has stirred up "debate". I can already imagine the kind of places different perspectives could take this. I have never been comfortable teaching from Scripture and then saying, "Here now, this is what you do". Somehow it feels like this is the task of the Church.

The same Scripture gets applied in various or contrary ways. It is often misapplied. After reading what follows, some might ask, "How did you get from this to that?" For the most part, however, this is precisely the nature of almost all application. It is like the old joke about people from Maine. When the traveling city people come up to Maine, they often have a hard time finding their destination because Maine is mostly a web of small towns. When the city person finally stops to ask a local how to get to a certain place, the local answers, "You can't get thaya (there), from heya (here)". What the Mainer is trying to explain is that there is no direct route to their destination. It will take some explaining to know how to get from here to there. So, I don't think I'll be doing much explaining of how I got 'thaya' from 'heya'. This will be more implications, reflections and even confessions than directives. I'm not aiming for a cohesive composition here. It will be more like a collage. I know that this study has helped me understand and find a rest in God. May God bless you and grant you his Sabbath rest.

Is There Such a Thing as a Day Off?

It would be great if the world stopped at least once a week for siesta. No doubt many of us feel dragged along by a hectic and non-stop pace. Indeed, some really like it that way and wonder what the huff is all about. Some may even think that rest is a rather frightening idea or just an excuse for laziness. When I was a kid, I remember going to the mall on one of the first Sundays they tried opening it for business. It was eerily vacant. Most people weren't ready for the idea that commerce had to keep going every day of the week. Now it seems inconceivable that most businesses would stop, not even for a moment. Factories run 24hours a day throughout the year. With E-business, shopping can be done non-stop. There is much that could be addressed along these lines.

It would be nice to institute a Sabbath, but it is mostly out of the question. This is true not just because the world we live in wouldn't go for it, but also because a good lot of Christians just couldn't do it without getting hopelessly bogged down in arguments about legalism. Even many Jews find it hard to keep Sabbath. I recently read a book about a Conservative American rabbi who related his struggle not only to get his congregants to observe it but also how much of a struggle it was for his own household. His wife felt more exhausted trying to prepare for the Sabbath than if she hadn't. Indeed, when it comes to the Sabbath, it takes more than personal resolve. It requires a community apparatus that supports it. The world I live in right now is in a season of change in which most of the sense of community is simply vanishing. It would take a considerable amount of resolve to rediscover a Sabbath.

More importantly however, let us remember that Sabbath is a response to God more than an opportunity to pick a fight with the world. Yes, it is in contrast to the 'gods', but only as much as it is primarily a response to God. It is because the created order is finished and God's redemptive activity continues, on the finished work of creation and Christ that we should consider what it means to keep the Sabbath. Otherwise, we truly will fall into the trap of the Pharisees in which the Sabbath becomes instilled with symbolism astray from its essential meaning. There is one thing Sabbath rest should teach us; it is best to fight off the gods of our day by mostly ignoring them, thus taking their power away.

So, maybe I wasn't that far off in my opening line when I said that Sabbath is something we have to know conceptually. What is required is a change of perspective, a way to view the world. However Sabbath 'looks' to us, it is a bold statement. It says God has the reigns on chaos. It declares that in God all things are good and destined for goodness. It also proclaims that one God, one earth, and one people of God are sufficient for all.

Can Rest Be Done?

It just simply is the case that the word Shabbat means to cease, and in order to experience rest as God does, then we must find ways to cease as well. In our world, it is not just about a day off; it is more about turning things off. We live in an automated society in which many things can keep working for us while we mistakenly think we're not. Ironically, everything that is perpetually working for us still requires a vigilant conscientiousness on our part. God knows how to turn it off, so we can too.

Turn it off:
the noise, the clatter,
the voice that says that everything matters.
Turn it off:
the TV, the radio, the VCR
the computer, the newspaper, and the car.
Turn it off:
the smiling image, and the thumping beat
demanding you be in the driver's seat.
Turn it off:
that way of seeing our plight,
as always a confrontation, a conflict, a fight.
Turn it off:
that compulsive need to see,
Your neighbor as your enemy.

The suggestion to turn it off may seem to some as a sort of blissful ignorance, a head in the sand approach. It certainly can be if the second and most important part is left out: turn it off and turn God on. Sabbath is God's gracious turning towards us, and it simply requires a gracious receiving from us. I am reminded of the response Jesus gave that swirling, busy, frenzied crowd who had worked themselves up into a high fevered pitch over a woman caught in adultery. Jesus ignored them first of all. He refused to get caught up in their manufactured whirlwind. I see in this response something pertinent. We have to learn in an age where we are instantly informed of a child's abduction on the other side of the world not to get all worked up about it. We think we can bring aid to these situations by our worry or by creating a target for our accusations. Much of this has to do with idolatry; an underlying belief in the insufficiency of our God and the ineffectual posture of prayer. God's Sabbath is a ceasing time. It is a time of cease fire and to kindle the fire of mercy and prayer.

Welcoming Shabbat

Our noisy day has now descended with the sun beyond our sight.

In the silence of our praying place we close the door upon the hectic noise and fears, the accomplishments and anguish of the week we have left behind.

What was but moments ago the substance of our life has become memory: what we did must now be woven into what we are.

On this day we shall not do, but be.

We are to walk the path of our humanity, no longer ride unseeing through a world we do not touch and only vaguely sense.

No longer can we tear the world apart to make our fire.
On this day heat and warmth and light must come from deep within ourselves.[75]

OUT OF THE ONE

Out of the One the many are blessed. This is just a slogan that I came up with. As it is stated, it is not found anywhere in the Bible, so I need to remind myself not to go too far with this. Hopefully, however, I have shown to some degree that this 'idea' is embedded in the Bible. It is so because it is grounded in covenant. Covenant is the thing in the middle, which holds the opposite ends in balance. It has helped me often to orientate my life around what's important. The extent I can orientate my life around God's view of the world is the measure that some of our anxiety is relieved.

"I think I'm turning Japanese, I think I'm turning Japanese, I really think so". Such was the lyrics of a popular song of the 80's. What does this have to do Oneness? Well, in a similar way, I think I'm turning Catholic. As I said, this may be more confession than application, so endure with me. I am trying to show how this teaching has affected me and given me a sense of rest.

I don't know what all it would mean to really become Catholic, but at this point in my 26 year Christian experience I'm sensing some real deficiencies in the way I've approached the Christian life. I became a Christian as a teenager with the guidance of the standard evangelical presentation of the gospel. I was taught to personally appropriate God's gift of salvation for my

---

[75] *Gates of Prayer*, pg 245 Central Conference of American Rabbis

life, to accept Jesus as my personal Savior and Lord. This was right and good; it did however, send me on a course in which I presumed that just about everything that had to do with God and me had to be personally pursued and appropriated. This is indeed closely related to American views of individualism as well as consumerism. Everything of God must be personally had. Just as we all must have our own stereo, lawnmower, tools, computer, car or whatever, so it is that we must personally have our own portion from God. As I experienced it, this meant that I alone had to understand the Bible, learn prayer, do good works, etc. Ultimately, what it meant was that I, by myself, had to determine God's will for my life in almost every aspect of life. I have lived a good portion of my Christian life re-doing, re-creating, re-examining, re-defining and re-interpreting just about every aspect of Christian life. I did this in a vacuum, as if the Church had not existed for 2,000 years who had with great pain, struggled through virtually every issue any Christian could face. Maybe this is just a problem with me (although it is, I also know that there was much in my Christian environment that lent itself to this), but I went about the Christian life as if it was my personal responsibility and necessity to reinvent the whole of Christian life, as if no one in all of human history had ever really done that before me! It sounds terribly presumptuous doesn't it? Yes, embarrassingly so. I traveled on a course of such anxious and endless searching. I caught a contagion that tended to see the Christian faith as a-historical. There is a black hole of faith from Jesus, the Apostles, and the close of the New Testament, to Luther, America, and my own interpretation of the Bible.

I have a very egocentric view of blessing. I think I'm the one to get blessing, not ever thinking that God's way is that for the most part blessing comes to me through another. As I rehearse the history of God's people in the Bible, I realize there are very few whom God has set apart to be the source of blessing. There is the seventh day, Adam, Seth, Noah, Abraham, Isaac, Israel, and then David and his descendants. Not even Moses makes the list. Only until you get to Jesus is there another One. The vast majority of others are not to look for their portion on their own, but from the blessed one. Contrary to a popular way of thinking, blessing – ability to thrive in goodness – cannot be personally appropriated by faith, good and hard work or perseverance. It is not an expensive item in a store, which we can acquire if only we acquire the resources. There is no immediate access to blessing. It is only through the blessed One that we receive our portion. Does part of our sense of being tired and restless come, not from the 'world' per se, but from our own distorted theology, which drives us toward a constant attempt to go after our own blessing? There is no immediacy to God's blessing. It comes from the Blessed One who is in-between God and us. Be reminded also, that it is not just Jesus alone, who mediates for us, but the covenant couple. The intermediary covenant is a union. It is One, but not single. It is Jesus in union with his Church.

I've had to seriously ask: Does the God of the Bible, work in and through mankind's history? Is there an essential and continuous solidarity between God and his people? For many years, I tended to see it as discontinuity. At least on the popular level, the history of God's people tends to be painted in a series of scrapping the old and starting over with a new and improved group. Unfortunately, this degenerates into smaller and smaller groups working in isolation. This is like gutting and then remodeling the whole house every time a guest is coming to visit or there's a problem with the sink. It adds a lot of extra work that is not necessary. The question of historical continuity, or what I call historical unanimity, also applies to the Christian view towards the Jews.

What I'm saying is of course complicated and complex. I can't deal with all of it here. I am advocating however, for a change in perspective, in thinking. As I said before, you may not agree with how I got from there to here. Remember that Shabbat is truly universal in scope. It affirms God's gracious turning towards all of creation and all of human history. It affirms that there is one earth, one humanity, one people of God, one salvation, and one God who is all in all. Jesus didn't abolish Sabbath. He extended it, not in some new and original way, but back to its original scope, all of creation, extending beyond just the covenant members. The tradition, in a time of desperation and protection, had set a course of limitation on the Sabbath. Sometimes in an effort to define our religious categories, we so limit it that no one, not even ourselves, can fit into it, like clothes that shrink every time you wash them. For me, I see in the Sabbath a real appeal to become Catholic, that is universal in scope.

Okay, what could this possibly mean? I will try and get practical. Well, do we all have to have our own worship? Being a musician and a leader, I've often been involved in leading worship services. I've been in on every kind of bickering and debate over what style worship should be. Worship has turned into an issue of preference, and is usually set in congregations haphazardly. This is far removed from the historical Church's concern and understanding of the importance of worship. The early church worked out worship in a pains-taking way over centuries. We on the other hand, assume it can be worked out willy-nilly, or according to who has the best musical abilities or the best songs. Do we have any sense of oneness being expressed in worship? The Jews, Catholics, and Orthodox do. What would it hurt to worship at a Catholic Church or to practice a Jewish style Sabbath? It is a real expression of understanding that out of the One the many are blessed.

Here I want to return to the mention of solidarity. It is true that Jesus redirected the meaning of the Sabbath away from that of his counterparts. But he did not cancel out the fundamental concern that Shabbat was an expression of solidarity. My understanding of Matthew 17:25 is that Jesus is not against every form or expression of unity with the people of God. The emphasis of the coin in the fish miracle is not on the miraculous as much as it is on the ease to which it could be done. Expressing essential unity with other believers is better than offending. If there is opportunity to show solidarity, then go ahead and do so. Just how much of my Christian life has to be spent resisting and opposing. Why do I have to be on a course where I have to have my own worship, my own little circle of understanding, my own building, my own agenda, own calendar? Shabbat affirms life not strife.

Is it possible for Christians to begin to seek solidarity? I know I'm dreaming and unrealistic. Why couldn't we have centralized worship? Why couldn't there be one celebration of the Eucharist? Why shouldn't it be the Catholic Church? The Catholic/Orthodox Church, for all its failings, has always carried the banner and held fast to the truth that there is only one visible, universal, and holy Church, and it has laboriously, meticulously, and historically worked that out and in the very fabric of its worship. It also literally and realistically has a universal apparatus already in place.

As I write, I can hear a thousand objections in my head, the number one being my own dreamy naiveté when it comes to the perilous inner workings of the Catholic Church. Perhaps at some later date I myself will laugh at such an absurd proposal. But let me say this, at least as it pertains to finding a real experience of rest as it is found under the Biblical rubric of Shabbat. I have spent a good portion of my Christian life (and I know I'm not the only one who has done this) resisting solidarity and working against the unity of Christ and his only Bride. I have strived more to distinguish myself from other Christians rather than to live in solidarity with them. This means not only with Christians that are around me, but with Christians everywhere, and with Christians throughout the centuries. When it is put this way, much of the Protestant construct becomes irresolvable for me. Perhaps it is time to end the protest.

For some readers I realize that his line of thinking strikes a deep cord. I could easily be accused here of stirring up anxiety, anger, and restlessness rather than rest. I wouldn't want that to be so. Even if one agrees with me that out of the One the many are blessed, and, among Christians, there is agreement that Jesus is 'the One', there is still vehement disagreement as to how that gets played out in a diversified and complex world. Certainly for many, the very claim to be a part of THE Catholic Church, THE Orthodox Church, or THE Christian Church is terribly presumptuous and does nothing to promote peace. Even so, I fundamentally want to appeal to seek solidarity with other Christians, and I'm saying this has a lot to do with finding God's rest. I need to stop equating separateness (holiness) with alienation and divisiveness with diversity.

Okay now, here are some suggestions for living into Oneness, historical unanimity, Shabbat, and rest. Attend a Catholic Mass or an Orthodox Divine Liturgy. There, one will at least associate oneself with the older historical expression of 'out of the One the many are blessed.' Even if you go to another church, plan to go once in a while. If you are a small group of Christians, instead of your own worship time, worship somewhere else. If you are a church, follow the historical Calendar of the Jews, Catholics, and Orthodox. (I know there are differences here, but it is generally the same, because the Christian calendar is intentionally parallel to the Jewish one). Consider adopting a Jewish type Shabbat (I'll say more about that later). Gather your family and friends on Friday night (and as Jesus suggested, a few of the lame, poor, insignificant, homeless, or lonely). Light the Shabbat candles, sing the Shabbat prayers, and give thanks for God's goodness. Eat, drink, and rejoice that God stops working and that his work is finished. Rest! Incorporate the Catholic Missal into your private and daily reflective life. Reflect and pray on what Christians throughout the whole world are. Incorporate Catholic, Jewish, and Orthodox liturgical elements into the worship that you participate in.

Let me now discuss another aspect of oneness on a much smaller scale. That is the union between a husband and a wife, and this being under God. It is imaging the union between Christ and his Church. I have been married for 18 years, but I do not speak as an expert. My wife could easily convince you of this. I have spent a good portion of my married life pursuing a 'committed' life in Jesus apart from a union with my wife. I was greatly influenced by discipleship models that are misleading when it comes to calling. If you choose to get married, then there is a clear-cut and nonnegotiable call. Live in union with your spouse out of reverence for Christ, because and so that out of your 'oneness' many can be blessed. Your marriage is a living covenant; it needs to be taken seriously. It is your calling as a disciple.

The role of parenting is especially important. It is a good, noble, and right calling in God that needs to be pursued with diligence and holiness. Perhaps some of the lack of rest that parents feel has something to do with chasing self-fulfilling and individual desires at the expense of their children. This creates restlessness throughout a household. Remember that as a covenant couple there is a Shabbat responsibility to make rest, not just take one. Men, I think especially, have much to turn around in this area. A lot of the male environment which we are familiar with promotes a reverse Sabbath in which we think our household exists for ourselves rather than vise-a-versa. We have much to learn in the area of setting our life aside in order to enable your household to thrive.

Here are some suggestions for promoting Shabbat in your home. Turn off the TV. TV is a powerful image-making vehicle and our kids are especially targeted. I actually feel that advertisements are more of a moral danger than the shows, or at least equally so. They provide a barrage of ceaseless wanting, and insatiable desire. They are restless reminders that our God is not sufficient and cannot help us thrive. Create a home of hospitality and warmth. Invite others to your home for meals. Have family meals. This, I have discovered, is absent from many people's homes now, so it needs to be suggested.

Be careful of recreation. Sometimes this can create a good lot of complication. For one, it should be re-creation not wreck-creation. In our society we are tempted with all kinds of ways to fill up spare time. It is easy for these activities to be consumptive, in money, time, and space. It can tend to leave us exhausted rather than rested.

RESPONSE TO THE FALSE – RECEIVING BLESSING

As I said earlier, Sabbath should be primarily a response to God, not a reaction to the 'world'; nevertheless, Sabbath rest happens through a separation from what is false. We underestimate the power that false-images play in our lives. We are under a ceaseless attack of insatiableness; even so, Shabbat teaches us not to deny desire, but to redirect it. Shabbat is not a time to spit on the world, but to emphatically affirm that, no matter what, God is in it. Rest comes to all who can say against the backdrop of hunger, God is enough. To affirm in our hearts, "enough," is to affirm the finished work of creation and salvation. God has both created us and saved us.

There is a big difference between true image and false image; it's the difference between fullness and emptiness, substance or the superficial. False image is the junk food of our spiritual diet. It has no real nutritional value. We can take in a lot, yet they do almost nothing to satisfy our true hunger. A false image never claims all-sufficiency. Indeed, it would be the kiss of death if it did. It would lose all its power. False images only claim to satisfy the most immediate longing. They do this fantastically well, and admittedly, an all-sufficient God, a God who is in it for the long haul, is not too interested in our wisps of lusty smoke that dissipate as soon as they appear.

The images of our culture lie to us,
      They need to be put away.

They keep telling us to go out and get our own blessing,
> Bless yourself, is their motto,
>> rather than may God bless.
They tell us to be filled rather than to fill,
> They keep telling us that we will die if we stop consuming;
>> Shabbat says we will live if we stop.
They say things aren't good enough;
> Shabbat says there's enough good for everyone.
The gods say take blessing;
> God says receive it.
The false images tell us that we can thrive on our own, alone;
> The True Image declares that we are made alive by a union of love.

MERCY, MERCY, MERCY!

My son often wishes that he would have more days off from school. This is mainly a complaint about getting up early on school days. For the most part, I think most people carry a similar wish. Indeed, I have demonstrated that Jesus' idea was to extend Sabbath, to have Shabbat more than once a week. We should understand Paul's discussion of 'all days alike' as agreeing with Jesus rather than a diminishing of Shabbat's importance. Jesus wants a boundless Shabbat. He wants the rest of God to go forth from the seventh day, just as Adam went forth into God's garden on it. Remember, Shabbat is a ceasing time, but not an ending time; in fact, it is a beginning time. It is the day we, in union with God, christen the week, and dedicate all of it to God's creative work. Does God wish that we experience rest everyday of the week? Yes!

The heart of Shabbat is mercy. To experience mercy is to know God's rest. Shabbat has always had its enemies. There are those who want to impose restlessness and perpetual work. They are willing to let chaos seep back into God's hollowed space. The antithesis to mercy is arrogance. Where arrogance reigns, merciful rest is snuffed out. To ask oneself, "how can I experience God's Sabbath rest?" is to ask, "Have people been merciful to me?" and "Have I been merciful to others?"

Can Rest Be Done?

Are people essentially good or bad? I don't think it makes much difference which side of this debate you land on; mercy in our culture is very hard to come by. It must be ever taught, and arrogance constantly resisted. We must learn mercy. We need to have the One true Image ever before us, allowing the pure and holy One to seep into our proud spirit. In the Orthodox tradition, there is a prayer called simply "the Jesus prayer". It is a short but potent prayer. It goes like this: "Jesus, Son of God, have mercy on me, a sinner." In this prayer tradition, the pious one is to repeat this over and over again, until it becomes the "prayer without ceasing", until it is woven into the very fabric of the soul. (In Shabbat, it is work that should cease, not mercy. Mercy should never cease). For reasons beyond me, we so easily turn the great and marvelous good news of the Gospel into a ruthless and ever demanding task-master.

I am coming off an 8 year experience of living in a closely-knit, intentional religious community. In many ways, it paralleled the *Chesedim*. Membership was granted based on the perception of the community that the one seeking it displayed an all-out desire to be totally devoted to God. Every member really did have an honest desire to live openly and completely for Jesus' way. Unfortunately, our well-intentioned community failed to recognize that what our Lord wanted was tender devotion not zealous devotion. It took on the fervor of a boot-camp rather than that of a household.

At one point in our degenerative crisis, another church offered their pastoral leadership. They came to us for a period of about 6 months to offer any assistance they possibly could. After being with us for some time, they came to a pathetic conclusion about all of us. There was no mercy here. I can't say how others dealt with that assessment; I was however, so caught up in a whirlwind of emotion, that I couldn't fathom what they were talking about. I certainly could see the lack of mercy on the part of others, but not so with myself. Even more so, it took awhile to recognize that mercy had simply vanished from this well-intentioned group. Our zeal had turned us into a ruthless and restless people. Activity snowballed under ever increasing expectation and intolerance for those who weren't keeping up. We would more often than not dispose of the weak or anyone who was in the way of our agenda.

We had become so familiar with each other that even our little quirks and foibles could not be tolerated. We were merciless, and consequently there was an on-going undercurrent of tiredness. We had somehow and unwittingly found ourselves back in the land of perpetual work. Ultimately, this has very little to due with time management. There was no mercy in our midst, and where there is no mercy there is no rest. We opted for clamor over clemency, zeal over gentleness, performance over tenderheartedness, and arrogance over humility.

I do not think that what happened with our community is an isolated incident. Mercy for the most part is an absent commodity in our society. Mercilessness fuels the restless fires of desire. We are in an arrogant and self-consuming nation. For the most part, we do not expect mercy. This is one reason why we seek to secure our own blessing (ability to thrive) rather than receive it from another; you can't rely on mercy. I believe Jesus really wanted his children to be that place and guarantor of mercy. He wants his people to be the place where anyone could come and find rest.

Transformation is needed on the most profound level and to the deepest parts of our life. How can I say one, two, three, here's how to do that. There is only one place one can go to find mercy and to learn mercy; it is Jesus. I love the part in the Catholic Mass, when we say before the reception of the Eucharist, "Lord we are not worthy, only say the word and we shall be healed."

The Great Litany of Peace

In peace let us pray to the Lord.
    Lord have mercy.

For peace from on high and for the salvation of our souls, let us pray to the Lord.
    Lord have mercy.

For peace, in the whole world, for the well-being of the holy churches of God and for the union of all, let us pray to the Lord.
    Lord have mercy.

For this holy church and for all who enter it with faith, reverence, and the fear of God, let us pray to the Lord.
    Lord have mercy.

For our civil authorities and all in the service of our country, let us pray to the Lord.
    Lord have mercy.

For this city, for every city and countryside, and for those living within them in faith, let us pray to the Lord.
    Lord have mercy.

For seasonable weather, for an abundance of the fruits of the earth, and for peaceful times, let us pray to the Lord.
    Lord have mercy.

For those who travel by sea, air and land, for the sick, the suffering, the captive, and for their safety and salvation, let us pray to the Lord.
    Lord have mercy.

That we be delivered from all affliction, wrath, and need, let us pray to the Lord.
    Lord have mercy.

Protect us, save us, have mercy on us, and preserve us, O God, by your grace.
    Lord have mercy...

...O Lord, our God, Whose might is beyond description, Whose glory surpasses all understanding, Whose mercy is without limits, Whose love for mankind is beyond expression; do You, O master, in Your kindness, look down upon us and this holy church, and bestow on us and upon those praying with us your abundant mercies and Your benefits. For to You is due all glory and honor and worship, Father, Son, and Holy Spirit, now and ever and forever.

Amen[76]

Celebrating a Shabbat

My friend and his wife, the one who originally asked me to write something on rest, taught me a great deal about Shabbat. It wasn't with any words, but by their deeds. As I said earlier, they were a part of our little group of leftovers, who were struggling to reorder their lives after a rather stressful and abrupt departure from communal life. We were all used to a well-ordered life with many set times and seasons as guideposts. Suddenly, we had little sense of anything set and orderly. I think this was especially true for my children who understood almost nothing of the reasons behind such a radical shift. My friend and his wife began a regular Friday night 'Shabbat'. She is Jewish with many relatives in Israel, and has spent time there. She especially wanted to have Shabbat like the ones she knew in Israel. They did this more for our sake than for theirs, and it was not always easy to pull it off every week.

I do not know anything about the Jewish celebration of Shabbat apart from this ad hoc experience, but I do know that I, and my family, came to look forward to Shabbat every week. It was very simple. It was a cross between a casual party and a dinner. It was very relaxing with no sense that anything

---

[76] Divine Liturgy of St. John Chrysostom

needs to happen. My friends always provided good food and plenty of it. They insisted this was in keeping with the spirit of Shabbat. Don't be chinsey. Just before dinner, we would light two candles, sing a simple Shabbat song in Hebrew, and toast our glasses. Then we would eat, relax, chat, laugh, tell stories, and laugh some more. Some would go home early. Some would stay late. For one evening of the week, we could simply celebrate the end of a busy week of work, good friends and food. We could simply celebrate our participation on the planet. Lechiam!

They would usually invite the same core group of people. We were all generally good friends and ex-members of the former community. We were used to being with each other, but not in such a serendipitous way. In our former lifestyle, we were used to a more committed life together which didn't always lend itself to a restful situation. They would also invite someone new or someone that was needy. Here, I am reminded of Jesus' parable that when you have a dinner don't just invite your friends, but those who can't repay you.

We kept our Shabbat tradition for only about a year. Then, we moved on. My friends didn't have the resolve to continue this little mini-tradition for an extended period, but for a season, this little happening on Friday night allowed us to participate in a little taste of our former and formal communal life. For me, however, something was gelling in my mind, as I was participating in our little makeshift tradition while at the same time studying the Scriptures on God's Sabbath rest.

Does community exist? My question is perhaps more weighty than it is meant to be, yet it is one that has been a personal and dogged search of mine. At this point in my life, I haven't been able to answer it. I'm not sure there are very many who would even bother themselves with such a question. Perhaps, as the days go on, more will begin to ask about this, because people are experiencing it less and less. In my own life experiences, I see a breakdown of community in almost every aspect of life. As an educator, I'm daily reminded of the lack of uniform values around raising children that whittle away at the ability to create a sense of coherence for our kids as well as us. I will not expound on this because I think that either one will have a nagging sense of this truth or otherwise not really know what I'm talking about. The normal elements of social cohesion, both good and bad, are dissipating before our eyes.

This is where I wonder if a stronger sense of God's Sabbath rest might be a little guiding light for us. For even if we feel as if we live in the most apocalyptic of times, or that the final eschaton is just around the corner, we can still pause long enough to affirm what God has affirmed from the beginning and will ultimately affirm at the climax of the last days. He has graciously turned to all of his creation. Ultimately, the Creator will give, not the kiss of death, but the kiss of Life. Indeed, the ones who don't believe that are the ones who fear stopping work long enough to celebrate the gracious gifts of the Creator. In the end, God will redeem everything. For those who don't embrace rest, it is "get it while the gett'n is good."

I know now that I cannot in anyway create community. We are all pulled in too many directions. The people in my neighborhood are not the same as those at work. The people at my church have no connection to those who live next to me. My social connections of hobbies, interests, and friendships are disconnected from my family ties and obligations. All of these pull on me. Not one of them seems to have the ability to hold the day.

Here is where I wonder if a little candle lit on Friday night, a little Sabbath prayer sung and said, and a little gathering of food, friends, and family can provide for many of us the hope and vision of a shared life in God. (Forgive me for being such a dreamer) A little Shabbat might go a long way. Even if it is only for a fleeting moment, and with some who you won't see again, it is pause long enough to say with God, "It is good."

Too many people that I know feel like they can't 'entertain' people because they are of humble means and don't have some mythical house that is more conducive for hospitality. We have come to a place in time when, even if it doesn't sound like much, it would be a noble undertaking to invite our neighbors over for dinner, let alone those 'in the highways and the byways'. But God never said we had to be rich to be hospitable or to entertain guests. The Spirit of Shabbat invites us, especially married couples, to graciously turn towards those around us, to be as rich toward others as He is toward us. This is what my friends, God bless them, have taught me about God's Sabbath rest. Don't just take a rest, make a rest, and in that, one will experience the goodness of God.

When my family and I moved back to Denver, we had to start over again. We had many old and new friends that helped us get back on our feet again. It took us many months to get even a sense of being settled. Nine months after moving, we were able to celebrate our first Shabbat since leaving L.A. It was a family choice to reestablish this little tradition. For our first Shabbat, we invited a couple of Christian families in our neighborhood. We lit the candles, sang a little Shabbat song in Hebrew, toasted our glasses, and said a Sabbath prayer. Later in the evening, our priest came by for a house-blessing liturgy. Everyone hung around for quite awhile. Some left early; others stayed late. It was an enjoyable and meaningful evening, and our guests enjoyed it. It was a welcome sign for us, that even in a shattered world like ours there still can be some set times to pause in grateful reflection of all the goodness that surrounds us daily. I've found that this little Sabbath celebration is a good excuse to invite all kinds of people of all kinds of persuasions.

Shabbat – Rest in a Life Ordered by God

The twentieth century issue of evolution has unfortunately sidetracked the prominent theological concern of the creation account. To be sure, the ancients were engrossed in profound issues, but we must understand that their issues weren't the same or framed up the same way. The ancients were concerned with whether chaos or order ruled. Which one would ultimately win out?

The design of Genesis 1 is to affirm that order would ultimately win over chaos, that the universe has design and purpose. It was written at a time when the people of God had experienced great upheaval, when the world seemed to be spinning out of control. All through history, people have experienced unnerving and radial change, when it seemed like the world, as one knows, is unraveling and coming to and end.

Many of us perhaps feel like we are in another time like that. I would even say that those times of massive upheaval are more frequent due to technology and other factors. Now, as in times past, we must return to the affirmation of what was beautifully and masterfully presented in the creation account of Genesis chapter one. This account, as examined previously, ingeniously weaves the elements of chaos into a coherent whole that is christened or 'capped' off by the seventh day. Sabbath is God's affirmation that life on earth can and will be ordered by God.

My life now seems more ordered by disorder, disruption, and interruption than by seasons and days of reflection, repentance and celebration. Realistically, the financial demands of our contemporary lives have taken us far beyond the 8 to 5, Monday through Friday regularity. It has also taken us far beyond any sense of social cohesion whether it is at home, in the neighborhood, at work or church. Many people must work odd hours. Disrupted and ever changing schedules are more the norm than the exception. Honestly, to have patterns of ordered, and meaningful time from the frenetic pace my world is setting seems to be picking a fight with the world, a fight that appears to be won by the world.

Americans work too much. We work without ceasing. Our days off are consumed with taking care of all the business we couldn't take care of during the week because our jobs consume all of that time. If we are one of the privileged ones, we will have earned a paltry two weeks of paid vacation. These weeks too are consumed with a piled up reserve of unmet business.

The Sabbath teaches us that it is not only a day off that is needed but also seasons of rest. I know I am merely dreaming again, for this will not happen. But this is precisely what the Sabbath envisions. Everyone needs seasons of time where they let the business of life "lay fallow".

Here again, I return to another reason why I'm drawn toward my growing interest and appreciation with the "historical" (for want of a better term) Church; that is liturgy and a liturgical calendar.

I've come to know and appreciate another side of the Christian experience which goes all the way back (uninterrupted) to the early church. It is found, in what is variously labeled, "Eastern" or "Orthodox." Taking these two terms in their essence will elaborate what I'm getting at. Another word for Eastern is oriental. The word orient literally means "to the east" and is accompanied by the notion that one finds his/her daily bearings by the rising sun. Orthodox means "right glory". Putting these two terms together gives us a notion pertinent to the discourse on Sabbath: that is being oriented to a 'right glory'. As with many Christian terms, this can have a presumptuous tone to it, but my appeal is to suspend that, so as to get at something fundamental. All believers in the One True God must find a way to orient their entire life towards the "right glory", the ultimate and truest reality. From the institution of the Torah by Moses and onward, the people of God have always done this primarily in relation to time, in the setting aside hours, days, and seasons in which to get our true bearings.

It is no accident that the early church essentially embraced the liturgical calendar of the Old Testament and the Jewish people. They were not reinventing anything. Liturgy is not to be understood as simply the addition of a few worship services in our otherwise secular living patterns; rather, the liturgical calendar is superimposed over and infused into our lives in a way that in fact overcomes it.

In a catechism of the Byzantine Catholic Church this understanding of time is well stated.

> *The existence of time reflects our limitation; it means that a human person cannot experience all of existence at once. Time marks the beginnings and end of our earthly life. The Greeks had two words for time:* **chronos** *and* **kairos**, *which some Fathers distinguished to represent contrasting aspects of the human experience of time. These authors identified* **chronos** *as the measurable aspect of time, the time intervals calculated by material devices. We often yearn to escape this boundary to be united with One who is eternal and*

> *infinite, the Lord our God. Yet God has entered time. Although immortal, He was born and died as a man. His life has now become our life; and His resurrection, our victory over death – a manifestation in time. By coming into time, God has given all time a new meaning.* **Chronos**, *the Fathers taught, is overcome by* **kairos** *(events or occasions) which means the "opportune time" for us, the "time of salvation." St. Paul proclaims the new time of Christ, "now is the acceptable time* **(kairos)**! *Now is the day of salvation!" (2 Cor 6:2)*[77]

As I stated earlier, Jesus intended the meaning of Sabbath to be restored and extended. Indeed, he equated himself with it. Jesus, his life, death, resurrection, and ascension, is the Sabbath Day. He is that opportune time, the day of salvation, and our jubilee. The liturgical cycles do not just remind us of these things; indeed they do more than cause us to remember and relive them. They cause us to be in union with them. They spiritually graft us into the very fabric of the gospel of Jesus Christ, into his very real and ongoing life.

The more I'm immersed in the daily, weekly, and seasonal liturgical life of the Church, the more I understand a deeper reality to it that corresponds to much of what I've come to understand about Shabbat. From the introduction of *day* as the first act of creation to the last act of creation, the Sabbath day, God has laid into the very fabric of our daily existence opportune times to orient our lives towards him.

Sum of all fears – Boredom

Recently a new movie came out called *The Sum of Fears*. It employs one of those story lines that derives its entertainment value by playing on our ultimate fear around the use of nuclear weapons. This is a real fear; however, I wonder if Americans have another phobia that equals it, one that is played out on a more day in and day out basis – the fear of being bored. God forbid that we should ever have a dull moment. When we ask, "What's going on?" we fear the dreaded response, "Nothing."

---

[77] Light for Life Series, *The Mystery Celebrated,* pg. 15, God With Us Publications

Perhaps no one fears "nothing" more than parents. Somehow, many of us have come to believe that it is our responsibility to provide a never-ending stream of activity for our kids. For sure, kids do have that propensity to fill in their dull moments with ingenious provocations of their siblings. But they also learn to fill it with something critical: reflection, contemplation, wonderment, questioning, observing. They learn to be comfortable with themselves. Parents need to learn to just say 'so'. When that dreaded cry issues forth, "Mom, I'm bored," just say SO.

Perhaps the compulsion on the part of our kids is intensified by the way they view the adult world. How many of us cannot turn off our computers or cell phones for more than a few minutes? How many children see the adults in their lives as ever evasive phantoms who can't quietly be with their children without an accompanying sound, visual, or activity?

Sabbath is and must be a ceasing time. It is a time when we cease from certain kinds of activities. If we attempt this, in some shape or form, then we must be willing to face into perhaps our greatest fear: nothing, boredom.

God Bless You

As I think back over this book, there are more things that I didn't cover than I did. Yet, I wasn't seeking to be comprehensive. It was a valuable study for me and I gained from looking at it. It is hard to imagine in our increasingly restless and violent world how someone could dare to incorporate God's Sabbath rest into it.

There is one simple thing that I've come to practice from this study. I understand now that God's desire is to bless. Shabbat is God's stamp of affirmation of all that lives. He desires all to thrive and good things to abound for all. This being so, I've begun the habit of wishing well for people by simply saying or writing: God bless you. This is a worn out statement, but only for those who don't mean what they say. I've come to believe that it means a lot.

To say, "God bless", means several things. It means more than wishing good luck because it is asking for and affirming that God be intentionally involved in helping someone experience good things. When the early patriarchs blessed their children, it meant more than hoping for good things to come their way; even more so, in the very act of speaking out a blessing it put it into effect. The blessed one was then destined for goodness.

Magical or not, I also believe something similar. Not that I'm a patriarch, but I don't have to be. I know what the Creator and Redeemer of all the earth wants and makes happen. He wants the earth to be filled with goodness. He wants it to be filled with life and not death. He wants his people to affirm goodness and fullness not bemoan the lack there of.

The criticism can be laid that saying "God bless" can be like the complaint found in 1 John. There the author warns his listeners not to just mouth words, like "I love you", and then do nothing to help that person if they are in dire need. This is not contrary to what was discussed earlier about making Sabbath not taking one. I've come to understand, however, my own limitations. In most situations, and ultimately, God is the dispenser of goodness. I cannot possibly involve myself with everyone I meet, but I can leave them with more than an empty salutation. I can remind and revive their call in God to thrive and fill the earth. It is to say, as many African Christians do, "The Lord is good all the time, all the time the Lord is good." It is asking the Lord to allow the person being blessed to see and experience the goodness of God, to grant them rest.

So, with this note I will close.

> *The Lord bless you*
> *and keep you;*
> *the Lord make his face shine upon you*
> *and be gracious to you;*
> *the Lord turn his face toward you*
> *and give you peace.*[78]

May God bless you. Shaloam Shabbat.

---

[78] Numbers 6:24-26

www.ingramcontent.com/pod-product-compliance
Lightning Source LLC
Chambersburg PA
CBHW070514090426
42735CB00012B/2783